THE SECRET

OF

DREAMS

Tales of Wonder for Children of All Ages

By

SHQIPE MALUSHI

New York, 2018

Cover Art *by*   Shqipe Malushi
Edited *by*   Eileen Mahood-Jose
Illustrations *by*   Diellza Gojani
Book Design *by*   Anila Jaho

FOR MY DEAREST NIECE

ARIANA

Whose Gift has Always Been

the Secret of Joy

NOTE

My dearest little friend, I wrote this book only for you, to thank you for all the moments of joy that you gave me. For cheering up my heart at times when it was sad, and sometimes confused and dark; for taking away my fears, at times when it was hard, and for giving me reason to hope, to dream, and to love.

Thanks for all your questions and your curiosity about life.

This book will be your book. It was our secret of telling stories and I wrote all the stories as I told them to you. These stories hold the divine secret of joy, because they were told to make you feel better before you went to sleep, or when your tooth ached, or when you were feeling scared.

When you grow up one day, you will know where to look when you lose the answers.

I hope that 'The Secret of Dreams' will always keep your spark alive and show you the path in your journey of searching for the secrets of your own life.

With deepest love,

Your Aunt
Shqipe (Halla Lulu)

CONTENTS

The Swan	7
Big, Old Wolf	13
The Tear	17
The Wind	21
The Ant	27
The pearl Necklace	33
The Frog	39
The Angel	47
The City of Lights	53
The Bridge	59
The Dream Catcher	65
The Moon	73
The Sea	79
Blue Night	87
The Bell	95
The Tree	101
The Horse	105
The Grasshopper	113
The Truth	121
The Secret	129

The Swan

The little swan was crying by the sea because all the other swans had gone south and it was wintertime, and it was cold and the waves were getting big. The little swan was wet and trembling.

From a distance Princess Jasmine was watching the little swan from her window.

"O poor swan, why are you crying?" she whispered to herself. "Aren't you afraid of the dark and you aren't too cold to be outside?"

"Jasmine, dinner time," her mother called from the palace dining room.

Jasmine rushed to eat dinner but she wasn't very hungry. Her thoughts were outside with the little swan.

She ate fast and thought to herself that she would sneak outside the palace and bring the little swan in, because she couldn't bear to see the swan frozen in the morning. But she would not say a word about this to anyone in the palace.

"What is wrong with you?" Princess Jasmine's mother asked her. "You seem very distant tonight."

"Nothing, mother, nothing," she answered abruptly.

After dinner Princess Jasmine rushed outside without telling anyone where she was going. She took with her a little blanket and ran to the sea without being afraid at all of the dark. When she came near the swan, she heard it crying and calling its parents.

"I want my mother, I want my mother," the swan cried.

"Come with me inside my palace, " Princess Jasmine said, "I will warm you up and give you soup to eat."

"But I want to go south where everyone is," the swan replied, "I am the only one lost here."

"You cannot fly alone to the south," Princess Jasmine said, "If they had all gone you, better stay with me, and when they come back, you can join them."

"But I am so little I may not make it alone until the Spring. What if they don't come back? I will die from sadness."

"No, you will not, because I will help you get strong," princess said.

Then she wrapped the swan in her blanket and brought it back to her room. Inside her room she made a small basket under her bed where the swan would sleep. She brought the swan breadcrumbs and soup and fed it. Then she washed it in her bathtub and put it in the basket to sleep.

That night she had a dream that she was flying with the swan.

Every day Princess Jasmine would take her meals with her parents. Then she rushed to her room to play with the swan. The swan taught her how to dance by opening its wings and flying. The swan taught her how to sing, and how to laugh, and how to act, and how to see the colors of all the seasons. They played together for long hours and Princess Jasmine forgot that she was lonely. But her mother was very worried about her. She noticed that the princess spent all her time inside her room. She didn't speak with anyone or didn't ask for anything anymore. The Queen was really worried.

One day the queen decided to find out what her daughter was doing behind the closed door. "I'll just peak through the keyhole and see for myself," she said to herself and approached Princess Jasmine's door.

Inside Princess Jasmine was laughing and drawing pictures of the swan that was hanging right above the door where the mother couldn't see it.

The queen, seeing nothing except her daughter talking to herself, became worried, sick.

"Jasmine dear," she said. "Are you all right?"

"Of course, mother I am just playing," she answered.

The swan then flew around the room and closed the keyhole with its wings, winking to Jasmine. When the queen saw something white moving about her daughter's room, then closing the keyhole she got very frightened.

"Oh my god, ghost, a ghost" she screamed. "Help, help! a ghost is in my daughter's room."

Princess Jasmine took the swan and quickly hid it inside her closet and placed some of her sweaters on top of it. The Queen and the servants hurried into the room carrying brooms and looking for the ghost.

"The ghost, the ghost? Where is the ghost?" everyone yelled at once. But they couldn't find any ghost anywhere.

"There is no ghost here," Princess Jasmine said.

"Oh you don't know what ghosts are like, " her mother Queen answered.

When they didn't find anything, they left the princess alone. Then she went to bed and the swan came and sat by her pillow and told her stories about swan land.

All winter long Princess Jasmine and the Swan spent every minute together, sharing their worlds and their dreams and their songs. The princess told the swan funny stories about her cousins who slipped on a banana peel at Christmas Eve, and about drinking father's punch and getting drunk, and about her Aunt Baballoo who made her laugh. The swan told her about flying and the sun and the moon and the blue waters.

They didn't even notice that winter had passed by. While the whole house was still looking for the ghost, spring arrived. Then the time came when Princess Jasmine had to go to school and leave the house. Even at school she would rush to finish everything, so she could get home and play with her friend the swan.

One day when the days were warm and sunny, the Princess came home and first thing she noticed was that the window of her room was open. She called the swan but no one answered, and she began to cry. Then on her pillow she found a white feather that her swan had left her. She came close to the window and looked outside, all the swans had come back and they were flying high in the sky. Then she noticed that they were trying to give her a message. What she read in the sky was written by the swan wings.It said: We love you Princess Jasmine. Keep dreaming, we will always be there.

She noticed her friend swan flying higher than all others and she waved to her swan.

"I love you too," she whispered and placed the feather in a very secret place.

So it is said that this feather holds all the secrets of love and friendship, and whoever finds it will be blessed with luck and with all those gifts forever and ever and ever.

Big, Old Wolf

He came down from the mountains one stormy night.

Knock, knock, knock, he knocked at Ariana's door.

"Who is it?" she asked from her cozy apartment.

"It's Big, Old Wolf," he answered.

"What do you want?" Ariana asked him, not opening the door.

"Please open the door. I am wet. It's raining outside."

"So what am I supposed to do?" she continued.

"I just want to talk to you," he said with a big meek voice, "Just open the door I am not a bad wolf."

"But you are a wolf," she said wondering whether to open the door or not. She was curious as to why the wolf had come to her door.

"I am only a big, old, wet wolf," he said. "I know no one else in this neighborhood except you."

"Are you the wolf from the mountains?" Ariana continued.

"Yes, yes," he said excitedly.

A big, old, wolf once met Ariana in the mountains when she was picking berries and he had talked to her. Ariana had convinced the wolf to change and be a good wolf instead, because no one loved a wolf that attacked sheep, or played tricks on the girl with the red hood. No one loved that wolf. He had promised Ariana that he would do that and they became friends. Now that same old wolf was in front of her door.

"What the heck, " she said, "I'll open the door."

So when Ariana opened the door, she saw the big, old, wolf dripping wet. She brought him in and threw him in the shower. Then gave him her long robe and slippers and made some tea for him.

He liked it right away.

"Listen, " he said, "can I stay here with you? You have a nice place!"

"No," said Ariana, "you belong to the mountains and I can't let you stay here. Remember, you are still a wolf."

So the wolf slept soundly that night because he was tired; and Ariana was tired too, but she couldn't sleep. "What if the wolf stays here?" she wondered. What am I going to say to my friends?"

When she came home from school the next day, she found the wolf sitting in front of the TV eating her food and smoking cigarettes. Ariana got very upset and asked him to leave.

"Oh, no, I am not going anywhere. It's too good here," he answered.

But Ariana thought fast. She wasn't going to let the wolf take advantage of her.

She grabbed the wolf by his ear and got him got out of the apartment.

"Ouch, ouch!" the wolf cried. "Where you taking me?"

She brought him to the diner next door. She asked the boss to hire the wolf and teach him to work.

"You can't live in the city without working," she said, and left him there.

The boss put the wolf to work and made him a dishwasher. Meanwhile Ariana thought: He will teach him a lesson.

So each time the wolf turned to sit and rest, he was buried with dirty dishes that had to be washed.

Days passed and the wolf lost weight. All he did was work and sweat, and began to cry. "Oh my mountains, oh my mountains. Why in the world did I want to come down to the city, why?"

At that moment Ariana and her friend came to the diner to see how the wolf was doing.

When the wolf saw Ariana he was so happy to see a familiar face that he dropped a full tray of dishes and broke all of them.

The boss got upset and fired the wolf on the spot.

"See," said the wolf to Ariana," I guess I couldn't make it in the city."

"At least you tried," she said, "What now?"

"Can I come over tonight? And then tomorrow I am going back home."

So Ariana, her friend, and the wolf went home and ate and laughed and watched TV, and then they told stories.

The next morning Big, Old Wolf left Ariana's home while she was still asleep and left a note on the

refrigerator door.
The note said:

Ariana, you are such a good girl, but wolf is a wolf and cannot change. So the best place for me is the mountains. And please be careful and don't try to change the wolves because they they... they...they... Grrrr... It's a secret.

Love
Big, Old, Wolf

The Tear

Little Tonya cried and cried and cried. She was alone and had no money to buy anything for Christmas. Her mother and father were working long hours and she was babysitting her little brothers and sisters.

"What am I going to give them this Christmas" she worried and her heart wept.

That night when everyone was asleep and all the lights were out, Antas, the magic spirit came down through the straight from the chimney near Tonya's bed. He had heard her cry, even in the distance and he decided to do something about it and help her out. This spirit had magic power to turn all the waters upside down.

He kneeled besides her bed and touched her cheeks, still wet from the tears.

"Little tear, little tear, you will turn now into a pearl," Antas whispered. "And whenever Tonya cries you will bless her eyes." He then touched her eyes and went back to the chimney and disappeared.

That night little Tonya had a dream that she was left all alone in the house and it was dark and cold outside. She was calling for her brothers and sisters but it seemed as if they had been swallowed by the wind. Tonya then cried in her dream all night long. As she cried her tears

turned into pearls and in no time all her bed and her room were filled with piles of pearls.

In the morning when Tonya woke up she noticed the pearls. "What is this? " she asked her mother in surprise. Everyone then gathered around her bed. " Pearls, pearls, pearls! Where did they come from?" They all talked at once in joy.

Since no one knew the answer they decided they would just be very happy for the pearls they had, and so Tonya took them all and placed them in a big bag. Soon she got an idea to make necklaces from the pearls. Then she also made earrings and bracelets, and she had gifts for everyone for Christmas.

Then she learned that every time she cried, her tears would become pearls. She didn't tell anyone about this but continued to make her necklaces and soon started to sell them. Each necklace she made also had a secret song that she would sing when someone bought it. And so in no time people bought more and more of her pearls, and she became a very rich little girl.

Since she never had any money before and her parents had always been very poor, she decided to buy them a nice house and not let them work so hard. After she chose a house by the sea, she brought her parents and her brothers and sisters there. They were so happy they couldn't thank her enough.

Then one day the prince who lived nearby heard some of the songs that Tonya had sung to people who bought the necklaces. The prince invited Toyna to the palace and asked her to sing for him. She sang for him and he was enchanted. From that day on he asked her to stay there and he wrote every song she sang.

When Tonya grew up, she became a beautiful woman. The Prince married her and they had a lot of children. He always kept Toyna laughing and singing. And that's how she never told him about her secret of her tears and the pearls. He never learned her secret and they lived a very long happy life. Her songs are sung even today, but one has only to listen when the gentle wind blows, because it is said that the wind stole Tonya's songs one night.

The Wind

Sunaka had been asleep when she was awakened by something banging on her window. That night she had had a pajama party with her two little friends, Aida and Nita.

They had been looking at the stones, and the colorful leaves, and the wooden objects that Sunaka had in her room. Then, after a big fat dinner and a lot ice cream and many cookies that they were not supposed to eat, their stomachs blew up like balloons.

Before falling asleep the three girls sat by the window holding their stomachs and staring at the stars, as if waiting from the stars to make them feel better. But as they waited, they fell asleep.

"Bang, bang, bang," Sunaka heard on her window.

"Who is it?" she whispered half asleep.

"It's the wind, the blue magical wind. Open the window."

"What do you want?" Sunaka asked.

"You called for me, didn't you?" the wind asked.

"I didn't really know that you would come," she said.

"I am here now. What is it you want from me?"

"I just wanted you to make me feel better."

"Are you better now?" the wind asked again.

"Oh yes, and wait until I tell Nita and Aida that you really came. They will never believe me."

"Why don't you wake them up and I will take you for a ride." the wind said.

"Where?" said Sunaka.

"Up in the sky where you can see the stars, and touch them, and even get talk to them."

Sunaka was all excited. And she woke up her friends and they were all very excited. They forgot to dress. So they hopped up on the wind's tail in their pajamas and went off into the dark sky.

The wind blew... feewyuu!... feewyuu!... up, and left, and right they went all the way to the sky. The three little girls saw how fast they were climbing into the sky and they were so afraid. They held onto each other trying not to fall off. Soon their little house looked like a little dot in the distance.

Then they entered the magic kingdom of the stars. Everything was scintillating in the sky and the stars lighted the sky. The stars were shining and had happy faces. They greeted the little girls and touched them with their light. The three little girls started to shine too.

And the wind blew higher and higher, and higher and higher. Nita slipped from his tail and started falling. When Sunaka saw that her friend was falling down, she asked the wind to save her fast. So the wind flew down again and placed Nita back on his tail. Then they flew higher again. Sunaka was not afraid. She loved the sky and the stars. But Nita and Aida began feeling cold and were afraid of falling. They wanted to go back home and go back to their sleep. They became worried about what their parents might say if they found out that they had flown so high, so they started bugging Sunaka to ask the wind to bring them down.

Sunaka, enchanted with the sk,y did not want to go back, so she whispered to the wind, "Help me, great blue wind. Leave me here and bring them back home." The wind was supposed to fulfill Sunaka's every wish, so he placed Sunaka on one of the stars and said, "Wait for me." Then he went and brought Nita and Aida home. The star then gently rocked Sunaka into the dazzling blue sky and sang to her old lullabies. She fell asleep and had a dream.

Sunaka dreamt that she was entering a crystal palace that was made of stars and each star knew how to sing and how to speak. As she walked the stars touched her with their magic wands so she received all their gifts.

But though she looked everywhere for the great blue wind and Sunaka couldn't find him. And then someone told her that the great blue wind was captured by the sea and couldn't come to save her anymore.

Sunaka began to cry. But the stars told her that they would make a long rope of stars and she could gently go down to her room holding onto them. So all the stars held hands and became a big rope, and Sunaka smoothly came down to her room.

That night Sunaka wept outside and went down to the sea and she yelled at the sea, and the blue sea seeing that Sunaka was angry forgot to look at the great blue wind and the wind escaped and went back into the sky.

Then Sunaka went into her room and fell asleep in her bed.

In the morning when everyone left, she found a little star stone shining under her pillow. And she knew that her journey was not a dream; it was true that she was with the stars and this was their gift to her. She then kept her secret forever.

The Ant

It was that tiniest gray ant that got separated from her colony. She didn't know where everyone had gone but suddenly she found herself in a long labyrinth looking for her family.

She walked and walked, and walked, but every little ant house was empty, and every cocoon was empty, and all the little streets that the ants had built underground were empty.

"Where could they have gone?" she wondered.

While she wandered under the ground, she thought perhaps it wouldn't be a bad idea to get above ground. She hoped that she would find them there.

As she made her way to the top of the ground she realized she was very tired. She didn't even notice that the place where she was coming out was right by the sea.

When she came out, a big wave came over and swept the little ant away. Then when the wave came back again, the ant fell off onto the foot of Tasha, who was sitting alone by the sea.

Tasha noticed an ant moving on her foot, so she picked it up in order to save it.

"Oh, you poor creature! You are so wet. What are you doing dancing in the waves?" she asked.

"I am lost," answered the ant. "I was looking for my parents. I lost them somewhere."

"Come with me, " said Tasha. "I'll introduce you to my parents and maybe they will tell you where your parents are."

Tasha carried the ant on her palm and sang to her. She told her how lonely she was and how she prayed every night to the moon to send her a friend. And now the ant had come to her as a gift from the moon. And she would do anything to keep the ant with her.

Tasha sat down at the table and placed the ant by her plate.

"You're late for dinner," her father said frowning. "Where were you?"

Tasha avoided answering his question and started sipping the soup fast.

"Didn't you hear me?" Her father repeated his question.

This angered the tinny ant. "Gee what a monster," the ant thought. "Tasha saved my life and he is yelling at her. I'll show him..."

The ant crawled fast to his side of the table and entered his sleeve. The father felt that something was tickling him inside his sleeve and started to scratch his arm. The ant crawled faster and faster up to his nose and in one jump entered his nostril.

The father was itching all over; he didn't know what had gotten into him. He jumped from his seat and jumped all around the table as if he were mad.

"What's wrong with you?" his wife asked. But he couldn't answer because he didn't know what had gotten into him, walking inside his body and his head, and he heard laughter.

The ant was tickling his nostrils and having fun picturing the red face of the father.

Then the father sneezed "Aphchihaa... aphchihaa!" and the ant flew out from his nose onto the table. No one noticed the ant except Tasha, who was dying from laughter looking at her father.

Tasha grabbed the ant and went to her room, while her father was trying to understand what had happened to him at the dinner table.

The ant and Tasha lay beside the window and looked at the moon. It was a bright evening and the sea was very calm.

"It's so great to have a friend like you," Tasha said, "No one ever stood up for me like you did tonight."

"But I am just an ant," the ant replied. "I am so small."

"But you made my big Daddy shake," she said.

Then the ant started to tell Tasha how her family built an entire empire under the ground. They had houses, stores, schools and everything big people had. Ants worked so hard every night and during the day they went above the ground and got the supplies that they needed for their life.

"I miss my family, " the ant said. "I just don't understand where they could have gone. All of them!"

"I can be your family," Tasha said. "We can play

together and we can be friends forever."

"But it's not the same. I am just an ant."

Then they both went to sleep. Tasha had a dream that all the ants had come back and they were looking for her friend. They climbed all over her house and were upset with Tasha. They had gone to the golden city and her ant friend had fallen asleep so they had forgotten her. Now the golden dust from the golden city had fallen on the ants and all of the ants had a golden glow, except for her friend. They climbed out the window and took her friend away from her.

The next morning when she woke up, she found her ant friend sleeping on her pillow. When the ant woke up, she asked Tasha to help her find her people.

So Tasha and the ant began their journey. They looked in the meadows, in the streets, the hills, the forests, the beaches, but ants were nowhere to be found. Then they ended up at the bottom of the mountain and slowly began climbing. When they came to a big cave, they heard a strange noise like the waves of the sea.

"What's that?" Tasha asked.

"I think I know!" The ant answered and went straight inside the cave. Tasha followed without thinking what she might be getting into. Inside the cave she discovered that the walls were covered with gold, and small bridges were hanging from one side of the cave to another. She saw houses with golden roofs, and small golden buses and her mouth dropped open.

Suddenly, thousands of ants came forward, just

like in her dream, and greeted them. Her ant friend recognized her parents and her brothers and sisters and was jumping of joy.

"What's all this?" she asked in awe.

"We built it," the oldest ant said. "We work very hard because we believe in building and not in destroying."

"Why did you leave our backyard?" Tasha asked.

"Because your father wanted to build a water fountain over our homes and that would have killed us. So we had to leave and find a new home. We built this overnight. And you can stay with us if you'll like, but you have to work." The old ant said.

"But I am just a child," Tasha answered.

"Ant children work too, so there is no difference between old and young. You can learn to build at any age."

Tasha suddenly missed her parents and was sad that she had to leave. She couldn't live in the cave.

So she said goodbye to her ant friend ant and to all the ants and promised to keep their home a secret forever. Everyone waved to Tasha and thanked her for bringing their child home.

"Hold me in your dreams," the ant friend screamed when Tasha was at the bottom of the mountain. "I will always come there to see you."

And so it was, whenever Tasha dreamt of her ant friend, she would come to visit her and they would spend time together, and Tasha was never lonely again

The Pearl Necklace

There was this little sad girl named Maya who had nothing better to do but sit by the window and whine all day long.

"I don't have anything I want," she would say. "And it's my mom's birthday soon and I have no money to buy her anything" or "Why can't I have a blue dress like Maria?" or "I want a bicycle like John's." She would go on and on inventing things to whine about.

Everyone was tired of her whining. So one day all the birds, ducks, and other animals in her neighborhood gathered and had a meeting.

Maya was becoming impossible and it ruined their beautiful days. They thought of the ways to get her out to play rather than let her sit there and whine.

They all agreed that the best thing would be to go talk to her and invite her to be their friend.

They all voted and the gray spotted duck was chosen got to talk to Maya.

The next morning the duck came by her window and, when Maya started her old whining, he opened his wings and, like in a dance, started circling around her to get her attention.

Maya looked at the duck in surprise.

"What is wrong with you?" she asked him.

"Nothing with me," he said.

"So why are you jumping for no reason?" she continued.

"Because you are always complaining about something for no reason."

So they went on and on and the duck tried to convince her that if Maya were courageous she would go outside and discover that the world is beautiful.

"It's miserable," she said. "Tomorrow is my mother's birthday and I have nothing to give her. How can you say that the world is beautiful?"

"Miracles can happen," the duck said. "You can make her a box from the tree branches, you can make her a pillow from leaves, we can lend you some feathers you can give her as a decoration. There are beautiful rocks down by the sea you can give her," he continued.

"No, my mother deserves the best, "she said. "And I can't give her the best."

So the duck went back to his friends and they again had a meeting. He told them that Maya was very depressed, and that she wouldn't go outside of her room under any circumstances.

"But why is she depressed?" the rabbit asked.

"Don't stick your nose into personal things," the skunk said.

"Look who is talking!" said the snake.

They were really concerned. The snake then decided to sneak inside the house and find out why Maya was depressed.

When night came the snake entered the house through an open window and started going from room to room but she found no one anywhere. Finally she heard voices from the living room. She slid along silently and looked inside. Maya was sitting by her mother's bed. Her mother was not feeling well and had a pale face. Maya didn't like her mother to lying in the bed all day long. She felt that if she gave her mother a special gift, her mother would get up. But she had no way of getting a special gift. Maya's Father was working in a distant city and he didn't have any money to spend on gifts. She was thinking every day how to make her mother feel better but couldn't come up with any solutions.

The snake read her mind and she knew that Maya's mom was only sick from anxiety. She could get up if she received a special gift that made her feel loved.

"Aha!" said the snake to herself, "I am a genius. I got inside Maya's secret and got the answer too."

The snake slithered back to her spot outside the house and told everybody about Maya's secret. Now they understood her better and knew that she wasn't whining because she was spoiled but because she wanted to help her mother. They decided to send the duck to Maya's window again to tell Maya that miracles can happen. But Maya didn't believe the duck; she was far too disappointed since her mother's birthday was the next morning.

The duck returned and told everyone how Maya didn't really care about miracles anymore and didn't believe him.

So after the meeting, they all went by the sea and called the red fish to ask him a favor.

When the red fish pushed his nose out of the water, the duck grabbed him by the head and held him outside.

"Look, red fish do us a favor," the duck said. "Give us a few pearls as a gift for Maya's mother."

The red fish was upset at the duck for holding him by the head, but he agreed that they had a good cause and he said he would help. Then the duck let the red fish go while they waited by the water.

The red fish went down to the bottom more than thirty times, and each time, held a pearl in his mouth when he came up to give it to the duck. When they got enough pearls, they said goodbye to the red fish and then they left.

They went next to to the trees and found silk thread hanging from one of the branches. The duck strung the pearls through the thread and made a necklace.

Afterwards each feathered animal pulled out a feather and they wrote "Happy Birthday" with feathers and placed the necklace on it. Then they brought the necklace and the feathers to Maya's window and left them there.

They sat underneath the window all night because they wanted to see what Maya would do when she saw it.

In the morning Maya woke up and as usual she came to her window to look outside. When she saw the shining pearl necklace on her window on top of the colorful feathers that said "Happy Birthday" she screamed: "Mother...mother...mother!"

Since her mother had never heard Maya screaming before, she thought something was wrong. She got up from her bed after a long time and rushed herself to the window.

"Look, Mother, a miracle! Look, a miracle!" said Maya, crying when she saw that her mother had gotten up from bed.

Her mother came by the window and saw the most beautiful pearl necklace lying on top of the feathers wishing her a happy birthday.

"Who brought this?" she asked Maya.

"I don't know," Maya answered.

At that moment all the birds flew high in the sky, opening their wings. Then the ducks and turkeys and rabbits and the snake all came out under the window and greeted them.

"So it's you who did this miracle for me, but how?" Maya said amazed.

They all smiled and walked toward the sea.

Maya's mother was so excited that she forgot to go back to her bed. She went immediately to the kitchen to bake a cake for everybody, and Maya went outside to play with her friends by the sea. She forgot she ever whined by the window because she never did it again. Maya, her mother, and all her new friends lived happily together each day and never doubted miracles again. The pearl necklace remained forever in their home as a sign of love, caring, and happiness.

The Frog

Only one frog was left in the pond near Mr. Heckman's house. And all day and all night it kept crying wee-wee-wee.

The noise was unbearable.

Mr. Heckman couldn't sleep so he took his cane and decided to go and find out what that noise was and where it came from.

"Gee, Mr. Heckman, " said the frog. "What are you doing here so late?"

Mr. Heckman was frightened because he didn't know where the voice was coming from.

"Who's talking? Who's talking?" he asked.

"Gee, Mr. Heckman, you don't know me?" the frog continued.

"A Ghost, a ghost!" screamed Mr. Heckman, and he stumbled over his own foot and plopped into the pond.

The frog entered Mr. Heckman's pocket and didn't move.

Now this frog was not like other frogs. It was a red frog with black dots. No such frog was ever seen before, and where it got its dots, no one knew.

Mr. Heckman came back to the house very angry. His clothes were all dirty, so he took them off, washed

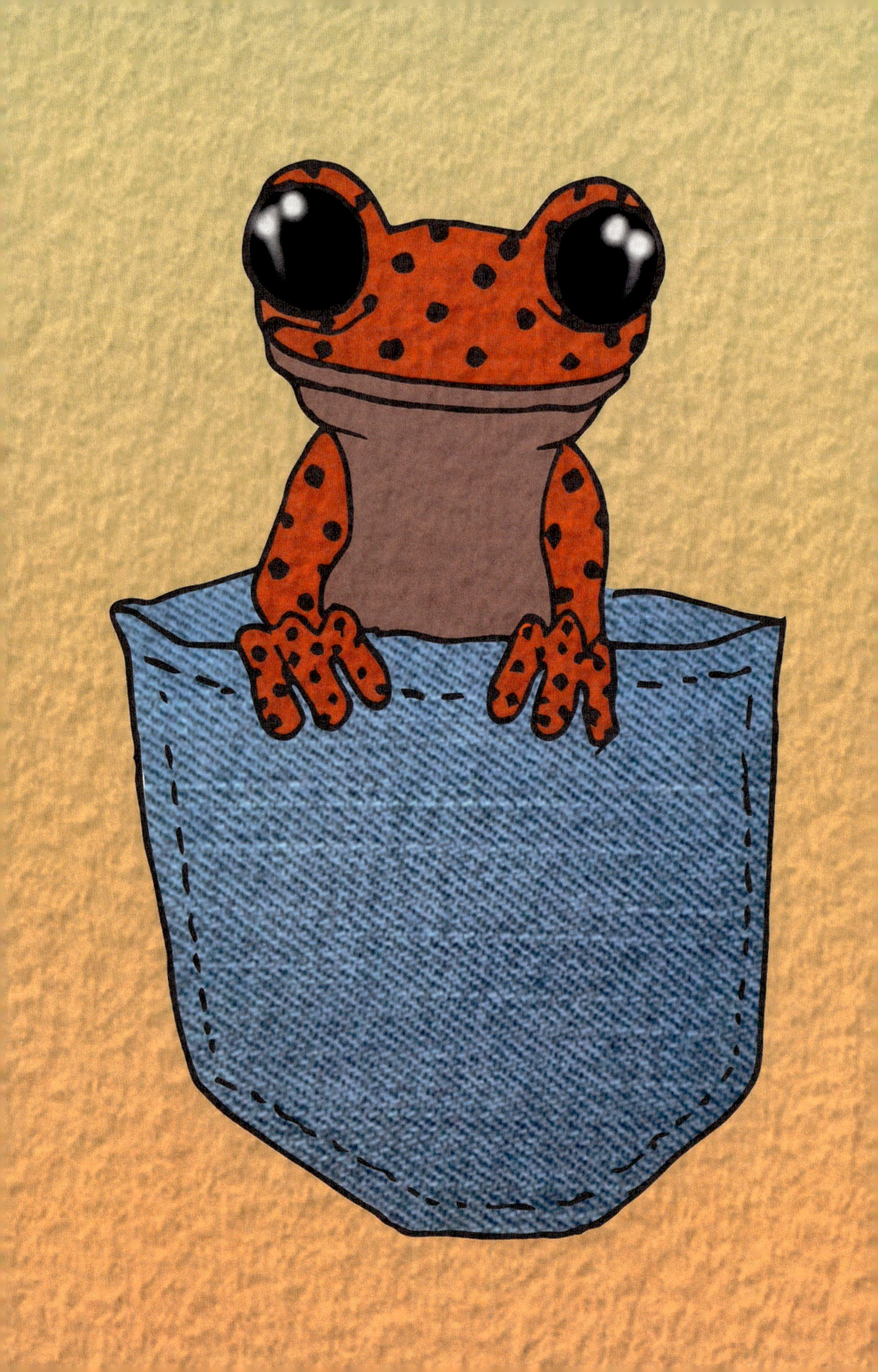

himself, and went to sleep. Little did he know that the red frog had come out of his pocket and followed him wherever he went. When he was sound asleep, the frog came from underneath his pillow and lay on his neck.

"Wee-Wee-Wee," cried the red frog. "I want my mother, I want my father. Wee-wee-wee."

Mr. Heckman thought that he was dreaming and in his dream he felt a nice hand touching his neck. He placed his hand over the frog, thinking he was patting a hand.

But the frog got scared and peed on his neck and wet Mr. Heckman. He jumped up, half asleep, not knowing what happened to him in the middle of the night.

So when he saw in the mirror that a red frog with black dots was tightly clinging onto his neck, he was very scared. He started yelling, "Get off my neck, get off my neck! Ah—Ah—Ah—!"

The frog was yelling, "Wee-Wee-Wee-Wee I want my mother…"

They both struggled until Mr. Heckman finally overcame his fear of touching the frog and he grabbed the frog and threw it outside the window.

The red frog flew straight back into his pond.

This time the frog was angry and he decided that he would get his justice.

He left his pond and headed straight to the forest.

"I will talk to the king of the jungle, and he will tell me what I should do about Mr. Heckman." After all, the frog thought, just because it's his pond that doesn't mean he has the right to throw me left and right.

"But you were hanging onto Mr. Heckman's neck," said his inner voice.

"And that's a little too much to ask, isn't it?"

"I won't mention that to the king," said the frog to himself and headed hop-hop -hop straight in the jungle.

It was a long, long journey to find the king. The frog got tired, then cold, and then angry.

On his way first he bumped into a rabbit who was so amazed to see the red frog with the black dots, that he froze on the spot.

"What's wrong with you?" asked the frog.

"You're not a frog," said the rabbit. "Only god knows what you are. There are no red frogs with black dots." And he went away without helping the frog.

Then the frog bumped into a turtle. "Would you help me find the king," asked the frog.

The turtle stared at the frog and said, "I don't know you. I never met you before. Go on your way." And she locked herself in her house.

Then the frog met the fox that touched her with her tail just to see if the frog was real. Then the frog met the wolf that tried his teeth on the frog's skin because he too disbelieved what he saw.

Then the days and nights went by, and the red frog was lost in the jungle and he saw so many different animals that he didn't even know their names.

One day the frog heard a sound he knew Wee-wee-wee. When he came upon a pond, he discovered so many frogs.

"Gee, I am home," he thought.

But when he came close, all the frogs popped their heads out of the water and stared at the red frog.

"Go away," they said, "you don't belong among us. We have never seen a red frog with black dots." They were all green frogs.

"Wee-wee-wee," cried the red frog, "but where do I belong?"

"Not with us, not with us," they all yelled in unison.

The red frog with black dots, broken hearted, went deeper into the jungle. He simply didn't understand why everyone was pushing him away. It is true that he was red with black dots, but he thought that everyone was red with black dots all over. He saw no difference in anyone.

So he walked and cried and walked and cried some more, and after so many days he finally met the lion king.

He waited four days before the lion king accepted him.

"What is the matter with you?" asked the lion king. "Have the butterflies been bothering you?"

"No, sir, not butterflies," answered the frog.

"Bees then?" continued the lion king.

"No, sir, not bees," said the frog.

"Birds then?" the lion king asked again.

"No, sir, not birds," the frog continued.

"So why are you here?"

"Mr. Heckman came and fell in my pond. Then I

went with him to his warm home, but he threw me out from his window back to my pond."

"What did you want at Mr. Heckman's home?" the lion king asked.

"I was looking for my parents," the frog answered.

"Where are your parents?"

"I don't know, sir," answered the frog.

"Let me think, " the lion king said and withdrew into his jungle.

He thought and thought and consulted his advisors, like the lioness and the tigers and leopards, but found no solution to this case. Mr. Heckman had a right to throw the frog out and he had a right to fall in his own pond. Because the frog was there and plus it was red with black dots, it wasn't Mr. Heckman's fault.

So after the meeting, the lion king told the frog what he thought.

"You've got to go back to your pond because no other frog family will accept you. You are the only red frog with black dots and you don't belong anywhere else. As for Mr. Heckman, be grateful that he lets you stay in his pond. As for your family, we don't know where they went."

The frog, saddened by this decision, headed back crying Wee-wee-wee-wee.

He didn't understand anything.

How could the lion king arrive at such a wrong decision? So what if he was a red frog with black dots. So what if it was Mr. Heckman's pond–he didn't do anything wrong. He actually always announced when the rain was coming or when something was wrong around Mr. Heckman's house. And he always made Mr. Heckman laugh when his friends came around.

So, thinking and rethinking all these the red frog with black dots walked the wrong way home. He never found his home no matter how long he walked. One day he spotted an old wise man and he told him the story.

The man listened to him then said, "My dear frog," you don't exist.

'I don't exist?" asked the red frog surprised. "How come?"

"You see," said the wise man, " It was a long time ago when red frogs vanished. And it's impossible for you to exist."

Oh, how upset the red frog was! It was not enough for him to be rejected, now he was told that he didn't even exist.

Now he was furious! He went straight back to Mr. Heckman's home, to ask for explanation and to tell him to stop bothering him with all kinds of nonsense.

When he came back, he didn't find Mr. Heckman there. The maid told him that no such man with that name lived there.

So the frog was confused. He didn't know what in the world was going on. First he was told he didn't exist and now Mr. Heckman didn't exist.

Then, all of a sudden the hand of a little boy named Joshua grabbed him and put him in his pocket.

"Wee-wee-Wee let me out." cried the red frog with black dots. "Who are you now?"

But all together, the red frog soon discovered that all this was Joshua's dream. That actually the red frog was green, but Joshua had painted him red with black dots before going to sleep, and so that's why the frog was red and had black dots.

This frog never had left his pond, nor had he lost his family, nor had he gone to the jungle. This frog was dreaming about his friend Joshua who had painted him red with black dots and took him away from the pond. When Joshua moved to the house next door, the frog thought his name was Mr. Heckman, who didn't really exist.

So like it was in their dreams Joshua and the frog met and became good friends ever after. The frog stayed red with black dots just for the heck of it. And Joshua kept calling himself Mr. Heckman just for the heck of it.

The Angel

The Angel fell from the sky one stormy night and got lost in our universe. As she was falling down the sky, tried to cling onto the stars but couldn't really hang onto them for too long.

So the Angel fell straight down onto the window edge of a little girl named Aurora.

Aurora was an only child. She was a very lonely child and her mother was so protective of her that she didn't leave her alone for one minute.

"Aurora dear, are you all right?" she would ask every minute when Aurora was home.

That night Aurora sat by the window and simply sighed.

"God, why can't I have a friend like all the other children? Why does my mother follow me everywhere?"

Aurora was asleep when the little Angel entered through the window, because it was open. So the little Angel looked around the room and saw all Aurora's toys, books, tapes, and pictures. Aurora was a neat kid and had everything in its place. The Angel then sat by Aurora's shoulder and looked at her pretty face.

"I'll wait for her here. Then I'll ask her how to get back to my world." the Angel thought.

"Who are you?" asked Aurora, when she woke up and noticed the Angel.

"I am a lost Angel. I fell from the sky and don't know how to get back," said the Angel.

"Oh! "said Aurora. "You don't have to go back. Stay here with me and be my friend. I need a friend."

"Oh! I need a friend too," said the Angel, and started jumping all over Aurora's bed. "I have a friend, I have a friend, I have a friend!"

Aurora brushed her teeth and got dressed, while the Angel sat on her right shoulder all the time. She spoke to her and told her all her secrets from school. She showed to the Angel her pictures, paintings, music box, and letters that her grandma had written before leaving for another world.

But what she forgot was to go down for breakfast and not be late for school.

"Aurora, Aurora, what's wrong with you today?" her mother yelled from downstairs.

"I'm coming, I'm coming." Aurora said. Then she turned to the Angel, "You can't come with me downstairs because my Mom will see you."

"Don't worry," said the Angel. "I'm invisible. Only those I want to see me will be able to see me."

So Aurora and the Angel came to the kitchen and sat down at the table.

"What do you want for breakfast?" Mother asked Aurora.

"A piece of toast," Aurora said. Forgetting that she

was in the kitchen, she turned to the Angel and asked, "What do you want for breakfast?"

"Cereal," Angel said.

"Cereal," Aurora said to her mother.

"Cereal or Toast?" Mother asked all confused.

"Both, Mother, both," Aurora said.

And Mother stared at her child, not believing her eyes because Aurora rarely ate breakfast at home.

As Aurora ate the toast, the Angel was eating the cereal. But what her mother saw was cereal flying to Aurora's ear and vanishing. She panicked and ran outside of the kitchen screaming, "Help, help, help, my daughter is eating cereal with her ears!"

But when her neighbor came in, Aurora had already gone to school, and the neighbor thought that something was wrong with Aurora's mother.

At school the Angel kept jumping from Aurora's shoulders to other children's shoulders. She kept picking up pens and erasers and throwing at them playfully. The children got restless and the teacher didn't know what had gotten into them. Aurora saw what the Angel was doing, so she jumped from her desk to catch the Angel, who was playfully escaping her hands. Seeing that Aurora was running after nothing, the teacher thought that something was wrong with her and sent her home.

As soon as she came home, Aurora went straight to her room and started to play with the Angel. Mother waited for Aurora to come down for lunch, but she

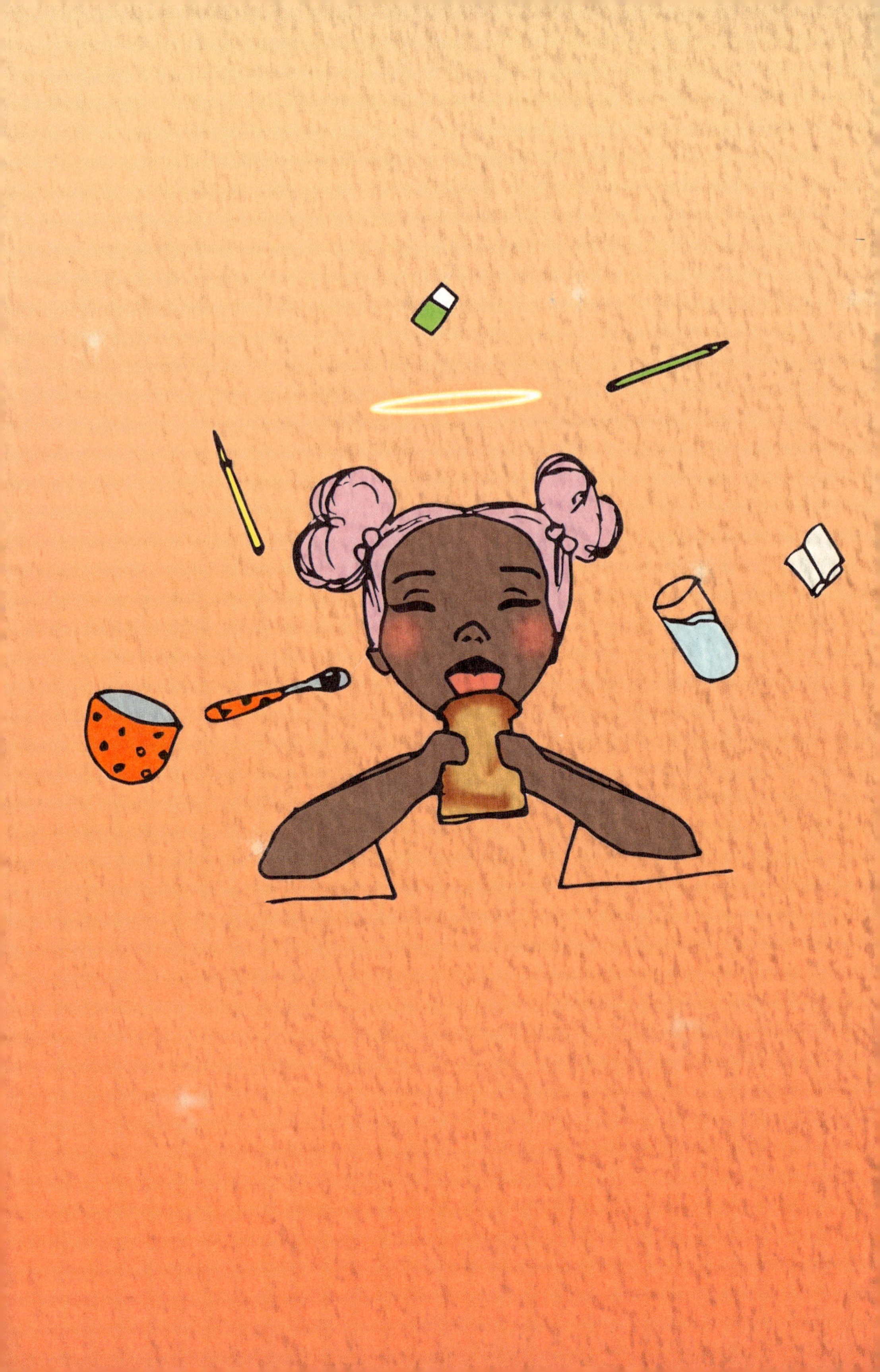

didn't. She got all worried and so she went to Aurora's room and peeked inside through the keyhole.

What a surprise it was to see a ghost sitting on top of her daughter's head while Aurora was drawing something. The mother got scared, picked up the broom, and entered the room without warning. She then started hitting the ghost with the broom.

Aurora screamed. The Angel jumped on Aurora's bed. The mother started chasing the Angel. The Angel hid inside the closet and made herself invisible, so the mother couldn't see her.

After an hour of chasing and seeking, the mother was very tired and gave up looking for the Angel, which she had called a ghost.

That night, when Aurora was asleep, a blue star fell from the sky onto Aurora's window edge. It came to take the Angel home and was twinkling. The Angel got on the star and they flew back to the sky.

But before leaving, the Angel scribbled on the window a few words for Aurora.

"I will always be your friend. When you are lonely, look at the sky, and when you just see the blue star twinkling; know that I am hearing you and I am near you."

Aurora read the Angel's message and never felt lonely again. She has seen the blue star twinkling every night ever since, before falling asleep, but her mother never knew about that. It was her secret.

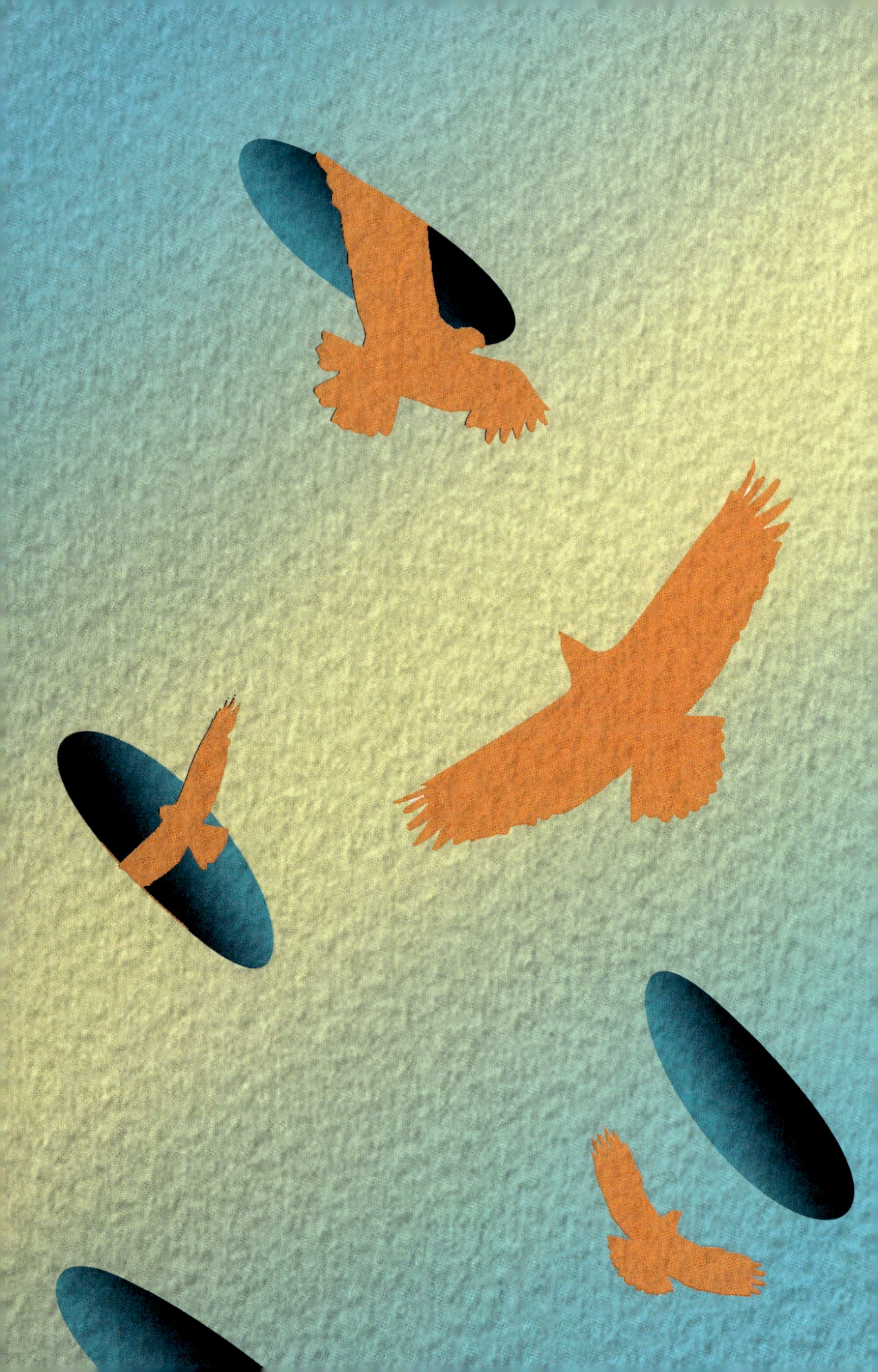

The City of Lights

The wounded eagle once fell into the forest. She was flying so high that the sun burned her wings. Feeling very dizzy, she fell down, not even knowing where. "Why did I fly so high? "She questioned herself, once she was on the ground.

She remembered that her grandfather had always talked about the city of lights that was beyond the sun. And that no one, until then, was able to find it, because no one could pass beyond the sun.

The city of lights must be the most beautiful city in the entire world the eagle thought and she started dreaming. Its bridges must be all golden and the forests and the seas all shining in the bright light. There should be plenty of fruits and foods for everyone, because everything grows and glows in the city of light. But the most important thing about that city, as her grandpa had said, was that the city of lights was made of love. There was so much love there and everyone was a pure light. Everyone could fly into and out of every world they wanted. They could enter the dream worlds, the world of winds, rains, thunderstorms and rainbows. One could play there all day long and never get tired. One could fly all day long and never want to stop. It sounded like a magic city where music was heard day and night, where waterfalls echoed like a symphony. Each drop of water gave a different freshness that could not be found anywhere else. You could see your soul in these waters. It was all true about this city, as eagle's grandpa had said. But it was a secret and how he knew these things no one had ever found out. But they all thought that he might have been the only one to visit the city of lights for a short time, so he could tell them about it.

As the eagle was recalling the city of lights, she heard a roaring over her head. It was the king of the forest, Mr. Lion himself.

"What are you doing in my kingdom?" he asked her.

"I fell down from the skies," she answered.

"Why were you flying so high?" he continued.

"It is my nature," she said.

Then Mr. Lion noticed that the eagle was wounded and he became merciful and decided to help her. He then called the forest doctor, Mr. Deer. And then he called his adviser, Mr. Owl. Then he called his carrier, Mr. Elephant, and the messenger Mr. Monkey.

Mr. Elephant carried the eagle to Mr. Lion's quarters, the most sacred place in the forest, where the birds sang sweet songs and all day long the waterfalls sounded like bells tolling.

It was green and fresh and beautiful in Mr. Lion's kingdom. He ordered that a bed be made of leaves for the eagle. He then asked some of his friends to bring fresh milk for the eagle, and bees to give her sweet honey.

"I am going to help you get strong again," said Mr. Lion. "We need you in the skies."

The eagle was very grateful, but she wasn't going to tell him about the secret of the city of lights.

So as it was told, the eagle and Mr. lion king became good friends. Everyone in the forest was nurturing the eagle and she was slowly getting strong again. She and Mr. Lion spent hours and hours talking and sharing their visions and dreams. He told her about the caves on his grounds, filled with music and dreams, about the wild rivers, about the fresh mist on the great lake that shines the eyes so one can see far into the night. He told her about his hunting and his loneliness. He opened his heart to her, and she forgot completely that she was an eagle; he fell in love with her.

The eagle too loved Mr.Lion. It was so good to be near such a strong king with a beautiful forest. She would be happy with him and follow him everywhere. She even forgot about the city of lights and her dreams, and her name. So what if she doesn't find it? She thought. Why should she be the one to be the first? The eagle completely pushed this thought out of her mind and stretched her wings. But she couldn't fly.

The rainbow, which had decorated her wings before going on her journey, took back her colors; the wind that had given her the strength to fly also pulled back his power. The moon that had given her the glow took it back. And the rain that had cleared her vision completely vanished. The eagle was very depressed.

Even though Mr. Lion was doing everything to cheer

her up, the eagle was getting more and more depressed.

"What is wrong with me? " She thought.

That night she had a dream:

Her grandfather came to her in this dream. He was tall and young and covered with a long robe of the rainbow colors. His wings were so large they reached the skies. He wasn't happy at all. He looked at his granddaughter, whose power was so small and weak, and said:

"You have forgotten who you are. Let me remind you, my dear. You are the eagle, the queen of the skies," he said. "You have lost your way and have forgotten your purpose. The city of lights is ours; it must be found and brought to the eagles. It exists so they can learn about love," he continued.

"But I love Mr. Lion, and I don't want to go to the city of lights," the eagle answered.

"The Lion is the king on the ground, and you are the queen of the skies. It was not intended for you two to be together. He must reign over the land and you must reign the skies. You must each find a companion of your own kind. You need an eagle to fly high and he needs a lioness to keep him down. So let go of him and come back to your truth."

The next morning the eagle told Mr. Lion about her dream. Mr. Lion was very touched by it. He called for a meeting with his councilors in order to find out its meaning. The councilors told him that he had to let go of the eagle because it wasn't meant for the two of them to be together. They were of different natures.

So if he didn't want misfortune falling on his forest, he had to ask eagle to leave. However, they told him that in spirit he could still continue to love eagle, and if she ever found the city of lights where everyone was the same, they could be together.

Mr. Lion came back to the eagle and gently asked her to leave.

"I was told that if you found the city of lights and bring it back to us, we could become one in the city of lights, where everyone is the same, and we all could love each other. It's only then that we could be together, but now you have to go back to your skies, if you don't want misfortune to fall up on my forest," he said.

The eagle was sad and happy at the same time. She too had made the same decision.

"I am an eagle, I almost forgot," she said and spread her wings. She was saddened to leave her sweet lion, who had helped her heal. But the fact that she could find the city of lights and bring it back to all of them gave her strength. Her wings had grown two times larger than she was, and all the animal kingdom had come to wish her farewell. Suddenly everyone noticed that her wings were shining and the colors had come back. They all knew that the rain, the wind, the rainbow, and the moon had returned their gifts to her.

Just before she flew into the skies, she heard the tiny voice of a little boy running up to her.

"Wait for me, wait for me?" the boy said.

He placed a golden ring on her small toe and wished her good luck.

"Bring us back love, "he said. "I know love is in the city of lights. I have seen it."

She had no time to ask the little boy where he had seen it, because everyone was singing the farewell song. She saw Mr. Lion wipe his tears of sadness. Then she flew high into the skies, making rounds of her dances until she became one small dot and vanished.

The eagle is still on her journey to the city of lights. It's a long, long journey and she has decided to take a different way than before. She will travel during the night when the sun is asleep, so he cannot burn her wings.

Everyone in the forest, including the little boy, is still waiting for the eagle to return. She will bring them love and light and freedom. The city of lights will have room for everyone and there will never be sadness or tears. Everyone will dance and laugh and celebrate. The little boy knew this, because the eagle came often to his dreams to tell him that she still had his ring, and that she would come back to bring it to him.

His mother never understood why her son always fell asleep by the window. This remains his secret of waiting, because he forgot to tell the eagle what his grandpa had told him about the city of lights. That it is buried deep, deep inside the heart and one didn't have to go beyond the sun to find it. But the eagle had flown so fast and now he hoped she would return soon. The city of lights was not far from home after all, but the eagle would soon find that out and come back home.

The Bridge

Tommy and Jerry always came back from school by the same route. They passed by the old church, peeked inside through a window, cracked a few jokes about the old priest, and ran away. Then they went to the cherry tree and picked some cherries and ate and ate and ate until they no longer could. Then they walked to see if there was some honey dripping off their favorite apple tree in blossom; if there was honey, they licked it fom their fingers, if not they ran further.

Their favorite secret place was the bridge by the River of Longing. They would stand on the bridge and throw down coins for wishes. Then they called the water spirits to make their wishes come true. They did this every day.

The bridge was old and not too many people passed over it. Many thought that any day the bridge would break and fall into the water, so they considered it dangerous to walk on; But not for Tommy and Jerry.

One day a rabbit passing by saw the boys on the bridge. He ran fast to the spirit of the winds and whispered that Tommy and Gerry were stealing dreams from the river. The wind got upset and blew very fast over the river. Since the wind didn't see them throwing coins, he believed the rabbit and tried to push them away from the bridge.

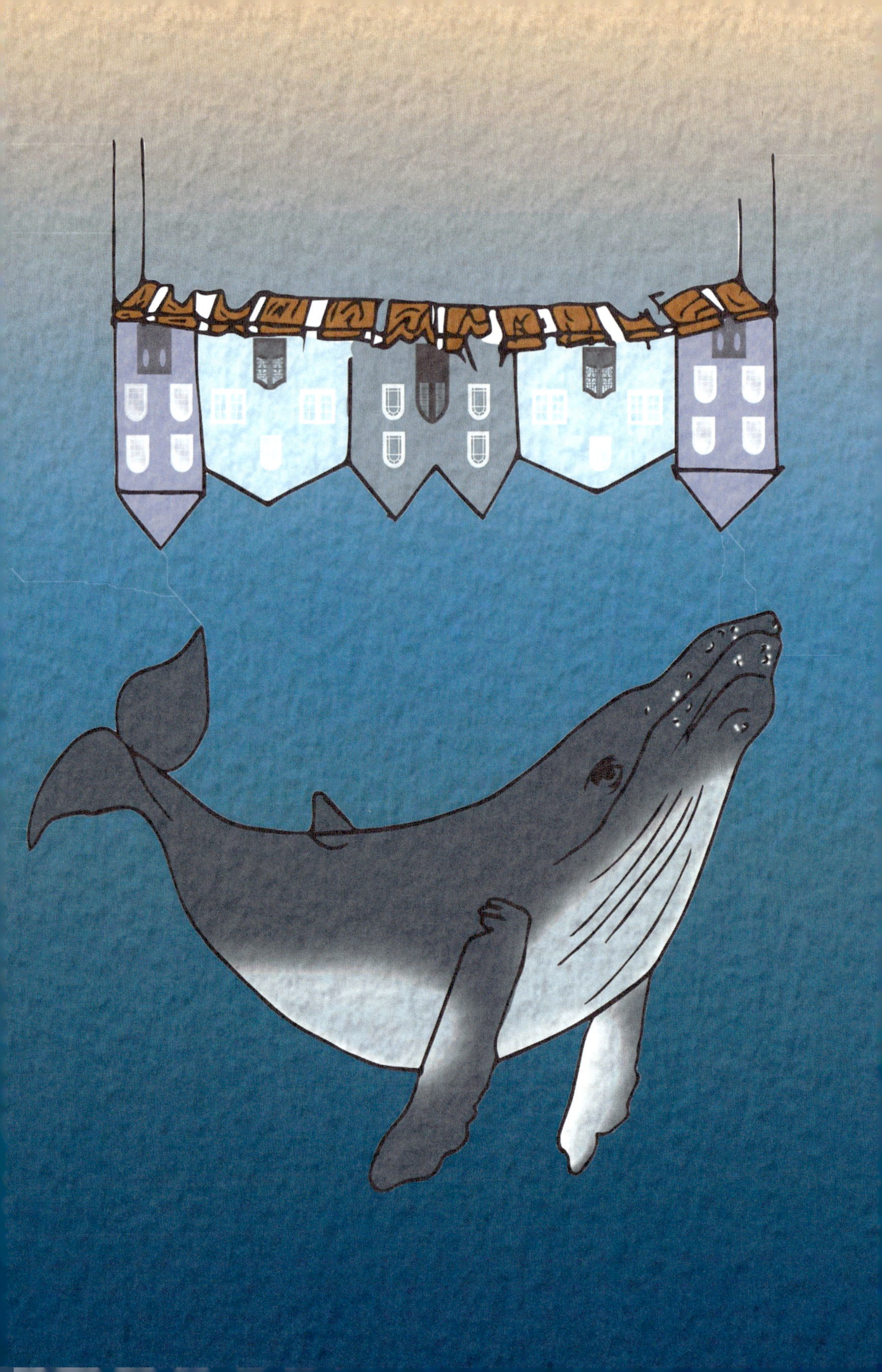

Tommy and Jerry held very tightly to the bridge, but they couldn't fight the wind, so they fell into the river. The wind then left and went back to his place, and Tommy and Jerry sank to the bottom of the river, with their stomachs filled with water.

As the water pushed them to the bottom, away from the bridge, they were unconscious and didn't know anything about themselves.

Darkness had fallen and their families were very worried, wondering why Tommy and Jerry did not return from school. They all went looking for them, not even thinking that they could be anywhere near the bridge, because they knew that no one ever crossed that bridge.

People looked in the church, and in the forest, and near the school, but they found nothing. As the night went by, the boys didn't come home.

Meanwhile Tommy and Jerry had gone to a watery world where no man had ever been. Deep inside the waters everything was made of magic rocks and crystals. There were plants and long stemmed flowers that never changed their colors, and were bigger than people. There were a thousand bridges of all sizes: golden bridges, silver bell bridges, crystal bridges, pearl bridges, grass bridges, and more. Their old, old wooden bridge stood right in the middle.

Tommy & Jerry noticed that golden light was coming from their foreheads and was lighting their way. They entered tunnels filled with white foamy clouds; they saw purple and turquoise gems, upside down ships and castles. They saw children playing silent flutes, and in front of them a ballerina as small as a kernel of corn was dancing. Farther along they saw fish talking and dancing. Some of the fish held meetings just like people. In fact they made fun of the people. One yellow fish had put a wig on her head and was imitating blond girls and everyone was laughing.

Then, like lightening, they saw their own village at the bottom of the river.

Their school was there, but upside down, so were the houses, and the church. They saw people walking on their heads and barely talking to each other. Even the Reverend Clark was standing on his head and preaching about how to behave and listen to your parents.

Tommy and Jerry didn't understand why the world was turned upside down. They sat down on a big rock to think what to do, how to turn the world the right way, when a big whale approached them.

"What are you doing, boys?" she asked.

"A whale in the river?" They jumped in surprise, "We want to straighten up our world," they answered.

"The world is as it is, not as you would like it to be. Instead of fixing it, why don't you just figure out what it is?"

Then she took them on her back and gave them a ride. She told them that she had lost her way from the ocean into their River of Longing and she was trying to figure out how to go back. They saw big green fields at the bottom of the river and other children playing soccer.

They saw faceless, invisible light beings in purple, blue, green, and gold colors moving like shadows behind each person. The frozen moon was locked under a glass bell, smiling. They saw so much more, the whole sky with the stars was down there and the sun was constantly moving. They were dumbfounded. It was then that the whale heard the people above calling the boys' names, and she threw them on top of the bridge.

The bridge then rocked them gently until they fell asleep.

Tommy & Jerry's Mom and Dad, the teacher, the priest and all their friends including the dogs Spunky and Misty, were calling their names. When they arrived by the bridge, someone noticed them and screamed: "Here they are, here they are!"

Everyone ran to the bridge and they bent to see if Tommy & Jerry were OK. When they saw them sleeping, they became upset. After Tommy & Jerry woke up, everyone was scolding them for going to the bridge.

"Didn't we tell you it was forbidden to go on that bridge? Look, it could fall down any minute," their parents said.

Tommy & Jerry didn't answer. How could they tell them that the bridge was their friend, and both the bridge and the river were alive? They had just been in the most magical world together. They mumbled something, but no one paid them any mind.

The next day the village people had a meeting. They decided that the bridge was too dangerous for the children and that it could fall down drowning them in the river, if they followed Tommy & Jerry's example. They called it a tragedy, and decided to blow up the bridge.

Tommy & Jerry were in school when they heard a big explosion. They didn't know what it was, but they ran outside toward the bridge. When they came to the bridge they saw there was no bridge anymore. Everything had been blown to pieces.

The thousands-of-years old bridge was now just the smoke going toward the sky. No one knew that the bridge had been children's friend and held all their secrets. It was on that bridge that they committed to their friendships forever. It was there that they kissed for the first time and threw coins for their wishes to come true. The bridge had been their beloved participant in all their games. It gave them dreams and it made them strong in their competitions.

"Why, why did you do this?" Tommy cried to the priest.

"We had to let the river free," he answered and his answer didn't make sense, because he didn't even know what was on the bottom of that river.

Tommy and Jerry then took a piece of the bridge home with them and decided to forever save the memory of the bridge in their secret world. Their lives went on, they went back to school, and they grew up like all other children. But no other child knew what they knew… that one-day they were going to find their old bridge and bring it back to their River of Longing.

The Dream Catcher

Mr. Harriman was an old pain in the neck kind of man. He was always very unhappy and very grouchy. All his neighbors crossed over to the other side of the street when they noticed that Mr. Harriman was walking towards them.

"Why is it so hot today?" he would say to his neighbors. "Why is it raining, why isn't raining? Why do you need a hat, or why are you wearing a yellow hat?" Once he said to a little boy that he had a tomato nose and a potato head. The boy started crying because he believed Mr. Harriman.

Even at Christmas time Mr. Harriman complained and, even though he would spend a few dollars for his nieces and nephews, he would constantly mention his gifts.

So day after day Mr. Harriman was becoming more and more difficult. Even his wife pretended that she was asleep most of the time when he was home.

Although he was a grouch, he was also a very lonely man. He loved music and when he was alone he would put music on and dance by himself. Then he tried to play the violin but again also only when he was alone. He liked to read children's books because when he was

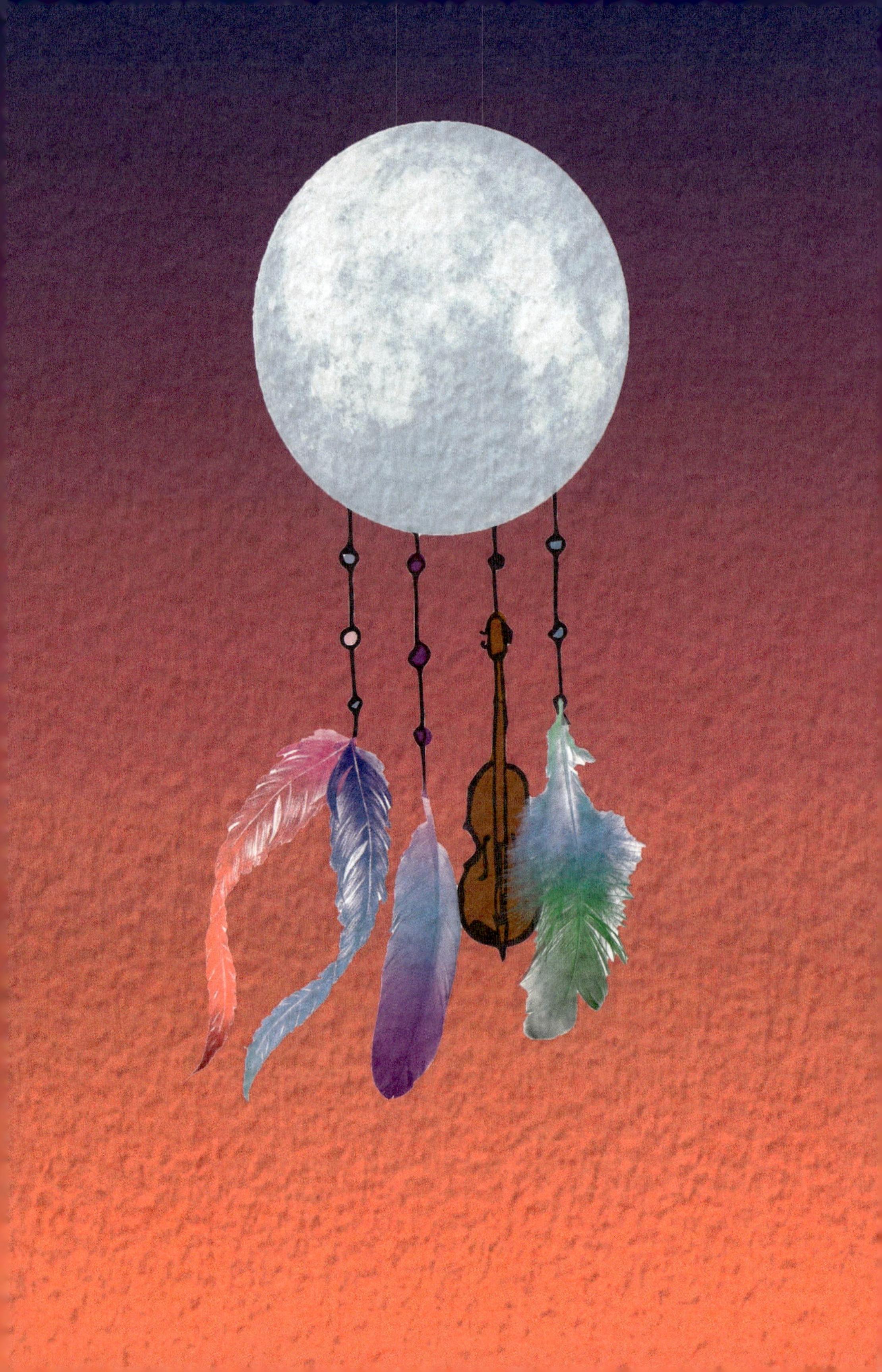

a child his father didn't let him read them.

"You have to know tools," his father had said. "Books are for girls."

So Mr. Harriman, even though he loved stories, he could never tell them in public, because he never believed he was good enough at telling stories.

One night Mr. Harriman got really sick and he was bedridden for a long, long time. Suddenly the street he used to walk on somehow became empty and people started wondering what happened to Mr. Harriman. They missed him because even though he was a grouch, he gave them something to talk about.

A little boy named Dennis and a little girl named Tina decided to go visit him in secret and bring him some cookies. They sneaked into his house and eventually they found his room. Mr. Harriman was snoring, "Aphu—-Aphu—-Aphu—."

They brought the cookies to his bed and started looking at him. He was an old man with white hair. Half of his teeth were missing, and his mouth was open.

"Get it, get it," Mr. Harriman started yelling suddenly in his sleep. Dennis and Tina became frightened and they thought that he was waking up. They knew if he found them there, he would yell at them. So they immediately went under his bed.

Mr. Harriman's talking didn't end there.

"I am the dream catcher, " he continued. "Here, sir, look! I have caught five thousand and five hundred dreams in my city."

"What's a dream catcher?" Tina asked Dennis.

"The man who steals your dreams, I think."

"How can anyone steal your dreams?" Tina continued.

"Through the chimney," Dennis answered.

And, as they were talking, they noticed Mr. Harriman's feet slip on his slippers walk towards the window. "I am the dream catcher," he said in his sleep. "I can fly through the night."

Then he opened the window on the third floor of his house and was going to climb outside.

Dennis jumped up and pulled him back in by his pajamas. Only then he notice that Mr. Harriman was a sleepwalker and he didn't know where he was.

At that moment Mr. Harriman woke up and stared at Tina who was coming out from underneath the bed.

"Who the heck are you?" he said to Tina.

Dennis, trying to make a joke, said from behind Mr. Harriman "I am the dream catcher."

"Ahh! You are the thief who stole my dreams!" Mr. Harriman said and started to chase Dennis around the room. Tina went back under the bed.

Finally Mr. Harriman locked his door and sat on his bed.

"You two are not going anywhere until I hear your story," he said.

Dennis and Tina told him the story about the cookies and how they really missed him on the street. Mr. Harriman was touched by the two children and asked them to be his friends.

"So," he said, "can we play a game?"

"What game?" Tina asked.

"You tell me," he said.

"Why don't we go to the street and tell everyone that Mr. Harriman has discovered a dream catcher. Then we will tell them all kinds of stories and see if they believe them," Dennis said. And so they agreed to play this game.

Dennis and Tina went down the street and told everyone that Mr. Harriman has discovered a dream catcher. Then all the people came to Mr. Harriman's door and begged him to tell them the story about the dream catcher.

Mr. Harriman brought his chair onto the porch, and asked people to sit down. Then he began:

"Once there was a lonely boy who had big ears. Everyone made fun of him and called him flip-flop. Flip-Flop did not have any friends because no one wanted to play with him. His ears came down to his shoulders and all the children laughed at him. So he spent most of his days in his father's shop repairing shoes. At night when he couldn't sleep he wandered, talking to the stars.

"One night a blue star asked him to come out and walk on the roof top, and this way he was to discover a magic world.

"So Flip-Flop went onto the first roof and peeked inside through the chimney. He saw a very old lady sleeping and her body was jumping in fear. Without knowing it, he entered her dream. He saw that someone was crying from an empty, burned down house, and the old lady couldn't get there. Then he saw horses galloping and almost running over the old lady. "Oh," Flip Flop said, "this lady is in danger!" So he took her dream with him on the roof.

"The next night he went out again. This time he saw a little boy crying and screaming, "Mother, mother!" But his mother couldn't hear him because she was covered with snow. So Flip-Flop became very sad and he took his dream away.

"So Flip –Flop, without realizing it, started to enter people's dream worlds and catch their dreams. He filled his nights like that until one night he discovered a beautiful girl sleeping and she was dreaming about a green meadow and waterfalls. There were deer and birds and squirrels and rabbits all around her. She was singing to them and they were all dancing around her. The girl's name was Amanda.

"Oh, this is a beautiful dream," he said. "I won't take this one, but I will be back."

The next evening he came back and saw that Amanda was alone in a frozen mountain and everything shone like crystal, and she was singing. Her song rang through the mountains like a bell.

"So Flip-Flop started coming every night to Amanda's dreams and he was so happy to be there. But each time he came, he brought with him someone's unpleasant dream and forgot it in Amanda's dream. This way

Amanda's dreams started to become cluttered.

"One night when he came to visit Amanda, who still did not know that she was being visited by a dream catcher, he noticed that Amanda was not feeling well.

"He came down the chimney and sat by her bed until she woke up.

"I am Flip-Flop," he introduced himself.

"I know you," she said "I have seen you in my dreams." And he was so surprised because he didn't see himself in her dreams.

"Why are you here?" she asked him.

"I don't see your dreams anymore. I am a dream catcher," he said.

"Someone stole my dreams," she said.

"So they became friends and he promised that he would tell her every night about the dreams of others that he had caught.

"This way he started to visit Amanda, not only on the roof but also in her room. She was the only girl who never made fun of his ears. And he told her all about the world of dreams and how he caught them.

"Amanda loved him and his story telling, and she couldn't wait for him to visit her. Now no one knew about this; it was a big secret.

"And what Flip-Flop didn't know was that Amanda was blind and she couldn't see him. He was so involved in the dream world that he completely forgot to see things in reality.

"One day they had grown up and Flip-Flop finally

asked Amanda to marry him.

"They got married and lived a happy life together. Flip-Flop was trying to make her happy and he was working very hard selling dream books, and dream catchers, dream gems, dream necklaces, and dream rings. He became a very rich man. This way, from stealing dreams, he managed to build a big factory of dream things and gave jobs to all his friends who used to make fun of him. He was so happy that everyone loved him. He also gave dreams to those who didn't have any. And little by little he became the best-known man in his city.

"However, he never noticed that his wife was blind and she never noticed that Flip-Flop had big ears. And so they lived happy ever after it."

Mr. Harriman finished his story.

So the people loved Mr. Harriman's story and they went home happy, wondering about their dreams and, a dream catcher whether could be stealing them.

The next day they all came again to Mr. Harriman's porch for another story. And little by little Mr. Harriman became a storyteller, something he had always wanted to do. He forgot he was a grouch and people loved him. Soon he became the most loved man in town and everyone brought him gifts and cookies in exchange for his stories.

Dennis and Tina kept their little secret that it was actually them who changed Mr. Harriman with their little game, and they too loved his stories and remained his faithful friends.

The Moon

Someone had painted the face of the moon red, and the moon was so upset.

"Damn it," she mumbled to herself, "who did this? I have a date tonight and now all my golden glow is gone."

She washed her face and just about when she was ready to go out on a date with the Sun, a few twinkle stars came by and asked her if they could help her dress.

The stars had fun with the moon because she was such a gentle lady, and so picky! She would look over her long dresses, not being able to decide which one to put on for a simple date.

"Let us decorate you with glitter," the stars said. "Let us put some makeup on you."

So they painted her face with all kinds of colors and drew her eyelashes long with the shades, and made her lips red like fire, and made her cheeks pink like peaches. The moon looked so beautiful, like a mirage.

Then they dressed her in a yellow dress and then jumped up and down on the dress, making it scintillating. The moon looked magical.

"Aha," the moon thought, "the Sun will fall in love with me tonight, and he will never be able to leave my sight."

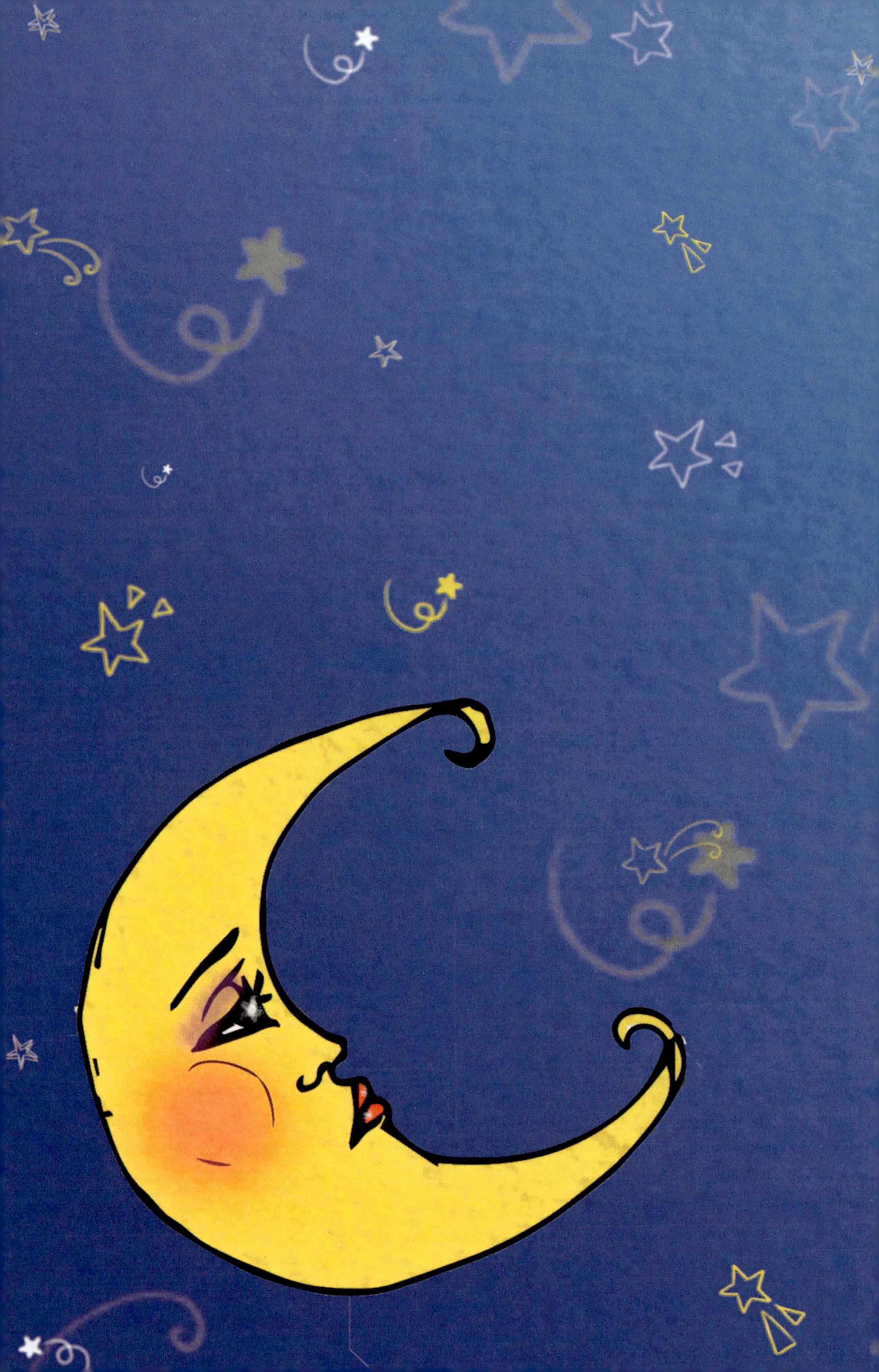

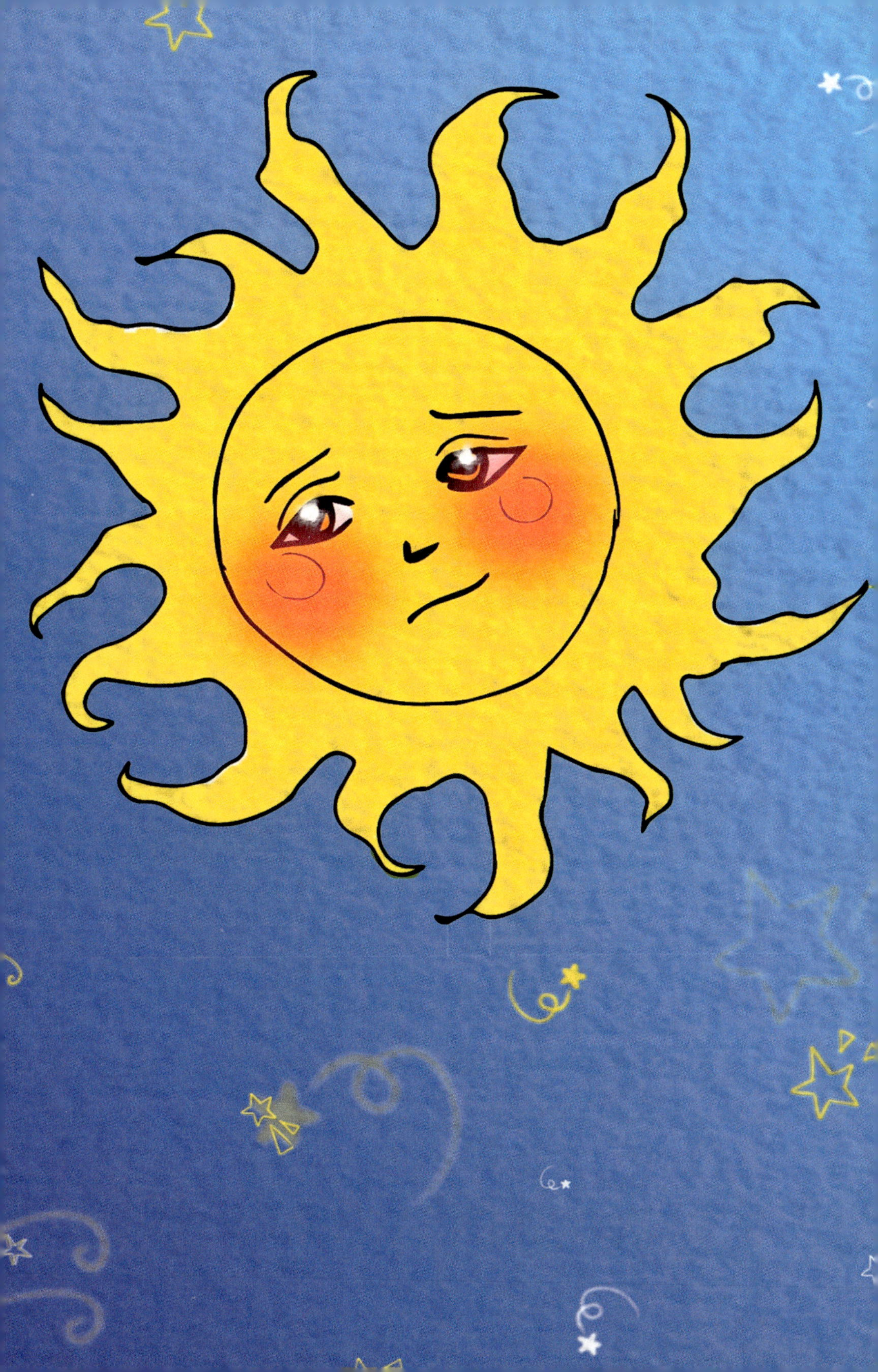

So, on the other side, the Sun was getting ready for his date with the moon and he was polishing himself. He sprayed his mouth with freshener, in case it had a garlic smell. He polished behind his ears, cleaned his nose, and combed his hair. He made sure he wore a white shirt with a clean collar and used nice strong cologne so he wouldn't smell from his own heat. He, too, was all ready for the date.

Actually the two of them were made for each other. They had the same size, the same height, the same glow, and the same depth. They both came from good families, mother darkness and father light. They both were very deeply educated about the universe, the stars, and human beings. They both liked music and to hang out. They had so much in common, except one thing. The sun was a day being and the moon was a night being.

She loved wandering around the night, reading, dancing, and staying up late. He loved waking up early and going early to sleep. What a good boy the Sun was. His mother was very, very proud of him. He never managed to go to the disco because the smoke bothered him and he didn't like alcohol. So he didn't drink, didn't smoke, didn't eat too much. He didn't do any of the things the moon did.

The moon loved to wash herself naked in the ocean every night. She loved to eat ice from the top of the mountains. She liked to ski and to swim and she liked herself when she won games with the stars. The moon visited Goddesses and had tea with them, and she played cards also. Even though the Sun was too boring for her, he was charming.

So they went on the first date and they chose one of best restaurants called The Star T.M. Five. The waiters with white gloves served them on silver plates and the music was gentle and lovely. A few stars fell like flakes, tingling their ears. Looking from the outside, one would think that they were madly in love with each other.

But as they ate and talked and tried to fascinate each other, the Moon drank a bit too much wine and she lost control. She was laughing so loud while trying to show the Sun how she can dance on one leg. She pulled her dress too high, so he got embarrassed. Then she just kissed him because she was feeling so sweet and she wanted to share her sweetness.

The Sun was so surprised; he jumped up in amazement and ran away, leaving her alone in the restaurant. He blushed and didn't know how he would tell his family what happened. They were old fashioned. They wouldn't understand such behavior. He was really upset. He would not call her again; he decided she was too much for him. But what could he do with his heart that was burning? She had stolen his heart.

Meanwhile the moon was in tears. She was left just like that, alone in the middle of the restaurant. What an embarrassment. Even the twinkling stars on her dress were sad for her.

So she went back home, washed her face, took off

her dress, and lay down on her bed and cried all night and all the next day.

Then, when the Sun didn't call her on the phone, she swore never to talk to him again. But what could she do with her heart that was aching? He had stolen her heart.

So as it was told, since they were not able to communicate well, they decided to avoid each other. The Moon went on one side of the world and continued her nightlife, and the Sun went on the other side in the daylight. And so she continues to bring light to all saddened hearts and make them feel better on the nights when it is dark and cold. He warms up everyone's heart when the day comes after a long night of dreams.

Some call her an old maid since she never married, and they call him an old bachelor. But the secret is that both of them are still in love with each other and they have never given up searching to find a way to meet and be together. However, the curse of separation still does not let them meet, but they will find a way one day, as long as they have the light burning for each other and it doesn't matter whether it is during the night or during the day. Their light will reach them and will bring them together. -

` It's an old, old, secret of love.

The Sea

All the town's people, east of the river, met to discuss the issue of Maria's heart. Somebody had stolen Maria's heart and had vanished into the night.

No one knew who it was or how it happened, except that one day Maria grew sick and pale and cried all day and all night. When people asked her why she was crying, she simply said; "My heart is no more, my heart is gone."

So her family and her neighbors decided that someone surely came one rainy night, while Maria was asleep and stole her heart. They tried to guess who it might have been but, as they went thinking the list of all the families, they figured everyone was an honest person and they could not have committed such a crime.

Maria sat there by the window looking at the moon and talking to herself. She refused to go downstairs to play with her friends. After all, she didn't want to share her secret with anybody.

In the meantime, the little thief with the deep green eyes, like the forest lake, that magically twinkled and for the long time, had stared at Maria, was running away with her heart. He was not going to give it back to her because she had made him mad. She had actually doubted that he could steal her heart, but then she was the first one to kiss him when he was so embarrassed about it. Maria has made fun of him, so he never believed that she cared about him at all.

One night, while Maria was pretending to ignore him, he stole her heart, without her even knowing, and vanished into the night.

After many days of waiting for him to reappear, Maria realized that he was gone, and so were his deep green eyes and her heart. It was then that she began to cry.

He, that deep green-eyed thief whom we will not name here because everyone might know him, ran and ran and ran to find a place for himself. He was running away from Maria's town and her people. He would hide somewhere, never to return. That way he would have her heart forever and it didn't matter to him that she was left without a heart.

Finally he came by the sea and the moon was shining in the dark night. He felt tired for he had run a long way.

"Why don't I rest here for a while?" he thought. "Then tomorrow I will continue."

He sat by the water and stared at the moon that wanted to know what was he doing with Maria's heart, but he said nothing in response. Then he stared at the waves that asked the same question, but he kept silent. He wasn't going to tell them that he, too, had wished to give Maria his heart, but she didn't seem to want it. Even though, he had begged for her friendship, after she said she didn't care for his deep green eyes or his friendship.

After staring at the waves of the sea and feeling very sleepy, he laid back and closed his eyes. He didn't know whether the sea was his mother or not, but he felt a warm wave covering him up. He felt tired and happy. Half asleep, he called "mother, mother, mother…"

Suddenly, he opened his eyes and found himself at the bottom of the sea. In front of him there was a huge castle with tall white walls. There was no one around. There was one only a bed with no one in it. But on it that read, "Leave Maria's heart here for now."

The little thief placed Maria's heart on the bed and began looking around. He heard voices. Farther down he saw a silversmith creating magical jewels from silver and pearls, but he worked upside down. He saw a horse, but it was swimming upside down. He saw Mr. Robins chasing his glasses that had fallen from his nose. Farther away he saw his father chasing some fish. He wanted to call to them, but no voice came out of his mouth. Then he noticed a red rope hanging from somewhere and he picked up the end of it.

The red rope pulled him away from the bed and from the castle. It brought him to crystal rocks that shone in a thousand colors all at once. There was music coming out of the crystal rocks that was unlike any he had ever heard.

"Where am I?" He asked himself, suspecting that he had gotten lost.

"In the land of magic," a wave whispered, pushing the water through his ears.

The little thief liked what he saw: glittering fish,

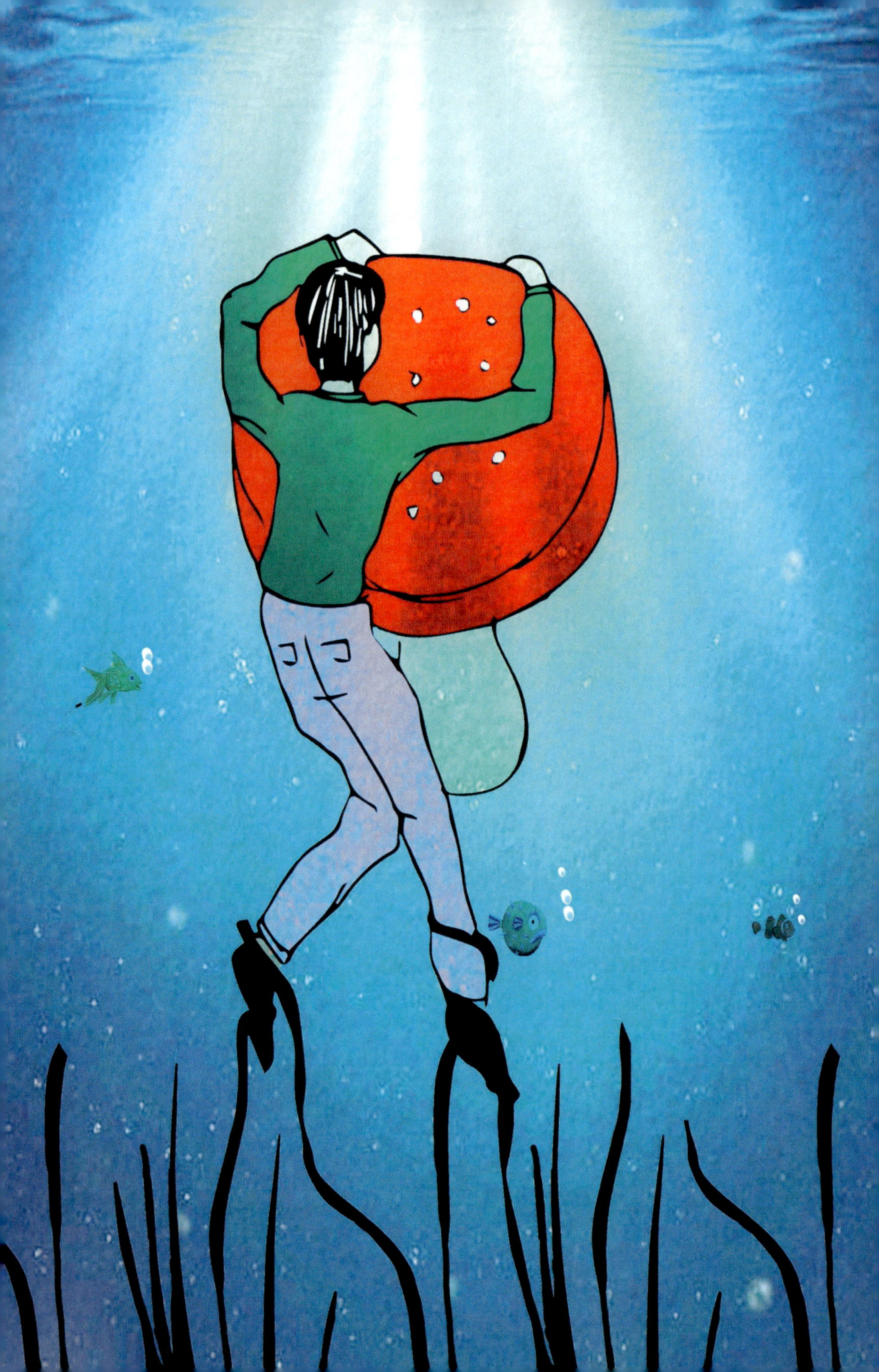

mermaids, old ships, marching green soldiers, talking plants, the face of the moon on the bottom of the sea, spider-webs, huge butterflies that looked like airplanes, and hanging bats. All that, and more, he saw, but he wished he were back up on land. He wanted to go home.

Suddenly, he remembered Maria's heart. He would return it to her because she would probably be sad and never be able to feel anything without it. But then he noticed that the sea had taken the bed away and he couldn't find her heart.

"What if some fish had eaten her heart," he thought. "Then no one would ever find it."

The little thief walked all over the bottom of the sea, but he couldn't find Maria's heart. He sat there crying and feeling miserable for having stolen it in the first place, and for having ended up on the bottom of the sea in the second place.

Then, as he cried last of his tears, he noticed a violet flame burning not too far away from him. The violet flame was magical, and it was changing colors from blue to green, to purple, to orange, to yellow and then to red. It grew bigger and bigger and it opened up like a hand. In that hand there was a little girl who looked just like Maria, and she was dancing.

He tried to reach the flame to tell her that he had lost her heart, but the closer he came to the flame it moved away from him. Then he noticed that, while chasing the flame, he came to a green field lit by thousands of candles. In the middle of this field, his mother was crying and calling for him. On the other side of the field, his father was doing the same thing. As he tried to go to them, a purple rain started to fall and it covered the whole field. He couldn't see his mother or father anymore. And now he was lost.

Just then he decided to turn around and go back, but the seaweed grabbed him and pulled him a thousand directions at once. His head ached as he struggled to get free. He would not have succeeded had a pink mushroom not come to his aid. The mushroom was big enough to cover him and help him float up towards the surface.

"Why are you helping me?" the little thief asked.

"Because we help everyone return to their worlds if they are not comfortable in ours," the mushroom replied. "But once you are in your world, you must keep it a secret that the sea is alive, and that we live here."

"Why?" asked the little thief.

"Because many greedy people would come to steal our treasures," answered the mushroom. "And because the sea, the mother of us all would not like that. She would get really upset and cover everyone with water."

The little thief opened his eyes and saw that it was early morning. The sun had risen and it was very hot and the little thief found himself wet on the beach. He didn't remember how he got there or what he was doing.

Suddenly, he saw a group of people running towards him. Among them were his mother and father. When his mother came close and saw that he was well, she scooped him up in her arms and gave him a big hug.

"I am so glad we found you," she repeated over and over.

All through the night the little thief disappeared, the town's people looked all over for him. His mother and father wept not understanding what had happened to their son. They couldn't possibly have imagined that he was the thief who had Maria's heart stolen. They looked for him in the forest, by the river, by the lake near the caves, under all the bridges but found him nowhere. Then they saw a mushroom floating in the sea. It carried Maria's heart. The town's people took Maria's heart and returned it to her. Maria was very happy to get her heart back even though she was very unhappy that the thief of her heart had disappeared.

Then everyone went back to the sea to ask their mother the sea where the little boy was. And, to their amazement, the sea had given them their little boy back.

It remains a secret how the sea took the little thief and showed him her depths, but since that time, the little thief has grown to be a silversmith who still gets his jewels from the bottom of the sea. No one knows how he gets them or where he gets them from but no one else has jewels and rocks like his. And, he has grown up to be a very rich and smart man. One day Maria came into his store to look for a ring for her mother's birthday. They were grown up and he still held the memory of her in his heart. So he asked Maria if he could walk her home. While they walked he told her all about their mother the sea and the world that he had seen beneath the waves. Maria was very excited to go there herself and see it.

"No, I can't show it to you," he said. "It's a secret and I promised to keep it."

But she was persistent.

"Only if you marry me," he finally said.

Two weeks later Maria was married to the silversmith, and one night he took her on a boat to the middle of the sea to show her the sea-world.

I don't know what happened after that, because they have not returned yet. Perhaps our mother the sea was upset that the little thief revealed the secret. If so their boat is lost. Perhaps they are both living happily ever after under the waves in the heart of the sea-world. Perhaps they are still traveling and discovering different worlds. Perhaps the sea finally united both of them their lost hearts are bound together for the rest of time. Who knows? After all it is a secret.

Blue Night

Little Jennifer had a dog named Blue Night, and every single evening Jennifer and Blue Night would go to her nanny's room. Her nanny knew so many stories and she would tell Jennifer one story each night.

The room where the nanny slept was very small and could only fit a bed, a dresser on which her children pictures stood, and a night table that always had a vase with fresh flowers. Around her room she also had books, shells, rocks, candles and so many other things. And every evening the room also held Jennifer and Blue Night would come to the room to lay down on nanny's bed. The dog was fat and barely moved, but her tail would wag slowly from side to side, as nanny told her story.

One evening Blue Night lay down on the bed and started snoring.

Nanny had never heard a dog snoring, so she was surprised. Little did she know that Blue Night had drunk a whole bowl of champagne that she'd be given, since it was her birthday. Blue Night was drunk!

"Wake up," cried Jennifer, pulling her dog's tail." Nanny is telling a story and it's rude to snore."

But Blue Night had fallen deep into a sleep.

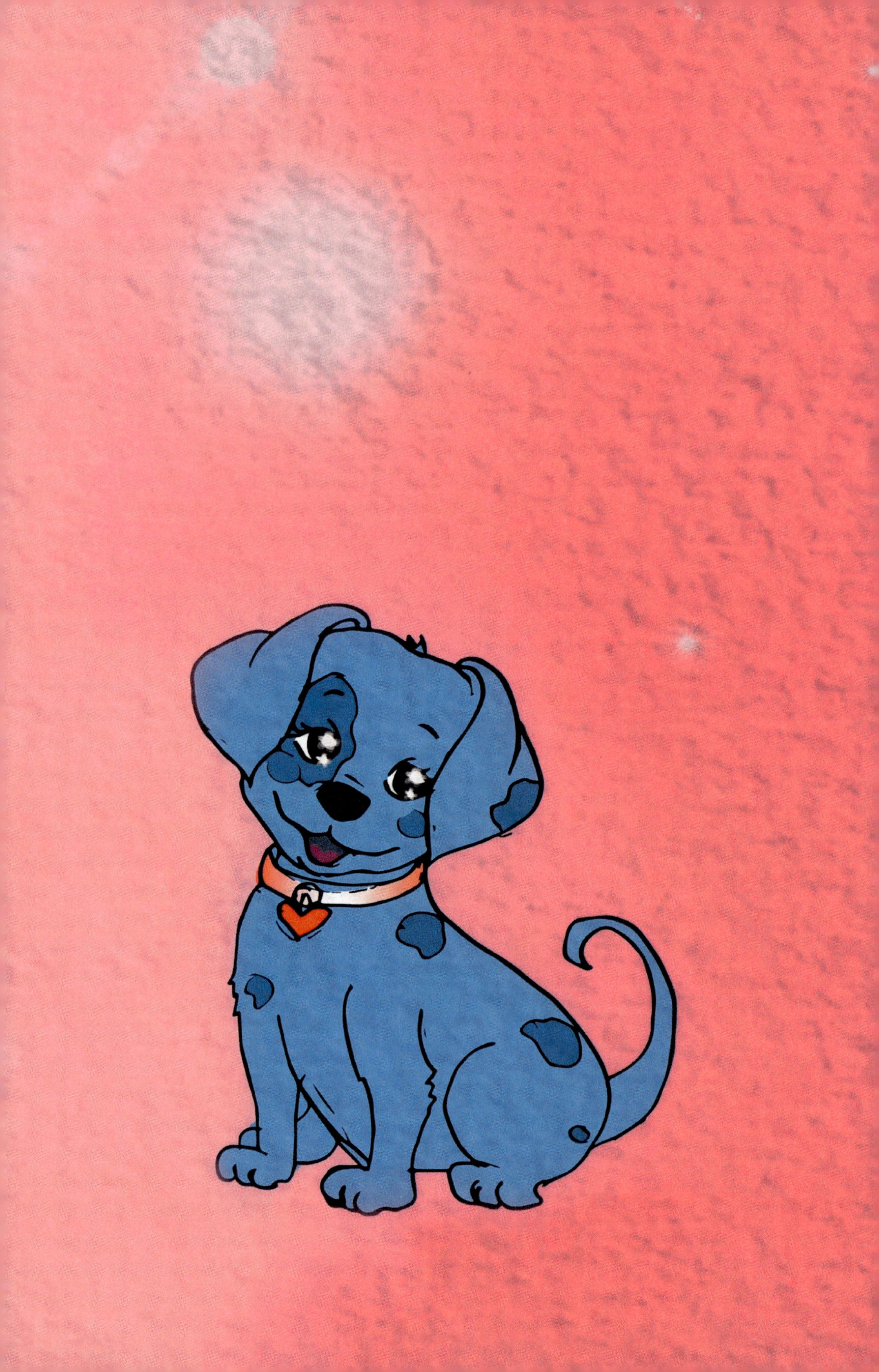

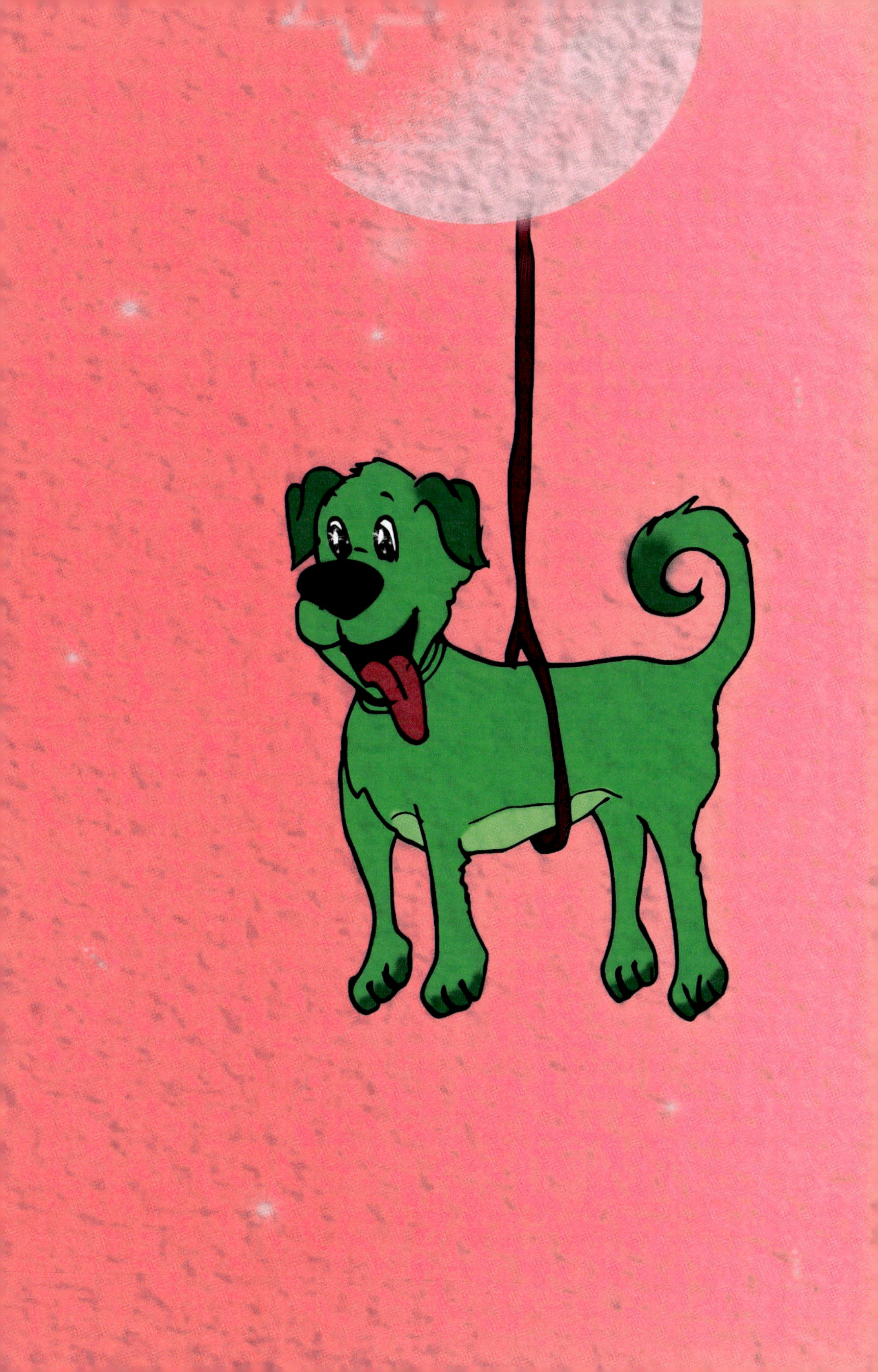

"Why don't we wait until she wakes up," Nanny suggested, and they both sat by the window looking at the moon.

Not only was Blue Night sleeping, she was having the nicest dream she ever had.

She dreamt that she was somewhere by the sea and the evening was warm and beautiful. The moon had landed on her tail and was giving off the nicest glow. She looked more beautiful than ever, especially with the moon being rocked back and forth on her tail. Suddenly, from out of nowhere came another dog, he was much bigger than Blue Night, and he was all green.

"What a nice green gentleman," she thought to herself.

When the green dog noticed Blue Night, he was fascinated watching the moon on her tail.

"I want to meet that lady dog," the green dog thought to himself. But just when he wanted to go and kiss her hello, he stepped in a pile of poop and slipped and fell flat on his face.

"Oh, how embarrassing!" he thought. " I could never introduce myself to her now. She will only laugh at me, and I will never be able to win her heart." So the green dog got up, turned around, and started to run away.

In the meantime, Blue Night had seen what happened to green dog. She laughed at first, but then she felt sorry for him. And when she saw him running away, she got angry. "What a wimp," she thought. She didn't want to let him go so easily, so she asked the moon on her tail to catch him.

The moon flew from her tail to the green dog's tail. Then she started pulling the two dogs towards each other. They came closer and closer together. Then Blue Night turned around and kissed the green dog, who immediately started melting.

"I am in love, I am in love," the green dog kept saying. "Your kiss is so sweet."

And at that moment the moon ran away, leaving them both, and went back into the sky.

Just when Blue Night began looking for the moon, she felt something pulling her tail.

"Get up silly. We've got to go," Jennifer said.

And so Blue Night slowly dragged herself from Nanny's bed and went upstairs with Jennifer.

When Jennifer went to sleep, Blue Night decided to go out. She was not going to stay there and forget the green dog.

So, she opened the door slowly and walked out. She was pretty sure that if she went by the sea and waited there, everything would happen, just like it did in her dream. The moon would come down from the sky to rest on her tail and then her green friend would show up and they would kiss. It would be so sweet. It was worth trying.

Blue Night left very, very, quietly, hoping that her dream would come true quickly, because she loved Jennifer, too. Jennifer was her long time friend. She remembered when Jennifer was a fat baby; she would roll on her stomach and giggle when Blue Night played with her tickling Jennifer behind the ears with her tail. Jennifer would feed her spaghetti under the table and her parents never knew. She baked Blue Night a cake for her birthday and let her eat it all by herself. Blue Night remembered that Jennifer loved her so much, she even tried to bake her a blue cake. The cake was blue, but it was so bad that even Blue Night couldn't eat it.

So Blue Night knew that she had to come back as soon as she found what she had dreamt of.

But when Jennifer woke up the next day, she did not find Blue Night. She thought maybe Blue Night had gone outside and was somewhere on the ranch with the horses and the snakes, but when she looked Blue Night wasn't there. She called for her everywhere but did not find her.

In the meantime Blue Night had arrived by the sea. When night fell it was cold, and she was hungry. She waited for the moon to come out for a long time, but the moon didn't come down from the sky to rest on her tail. Nights passed like that, and no green dog appeared. So Blue Night got tired of waiting and decided to go back home.

Oh! But Blue Night wasn't sure if she remembered the way she had come, so she was lost. I don't know if she ever found her way home, but Jennifer often dreams of Blue Night. She sees her waiting on the beach with the moon swinging on her tail. She sees her running in the waves coming towards her. She misses her dog… And even her Nanny's tales are not as much fun without

Blue Night's tail hitting against her lap.

It is said that the two of them are still looking for each other. Blue Night has learned that the moon can come to you no matter where you live, so you don't have to go far to search for her. As far as the green dog is concerned, he too could have been right next-door but she just didn't know it. So who knows? Perhaps Jennifer and Blue Night will meet again one day and the two of them will have many stories to tell each other. Until then, they will carry the hope in their hearts and keep their love a secret.

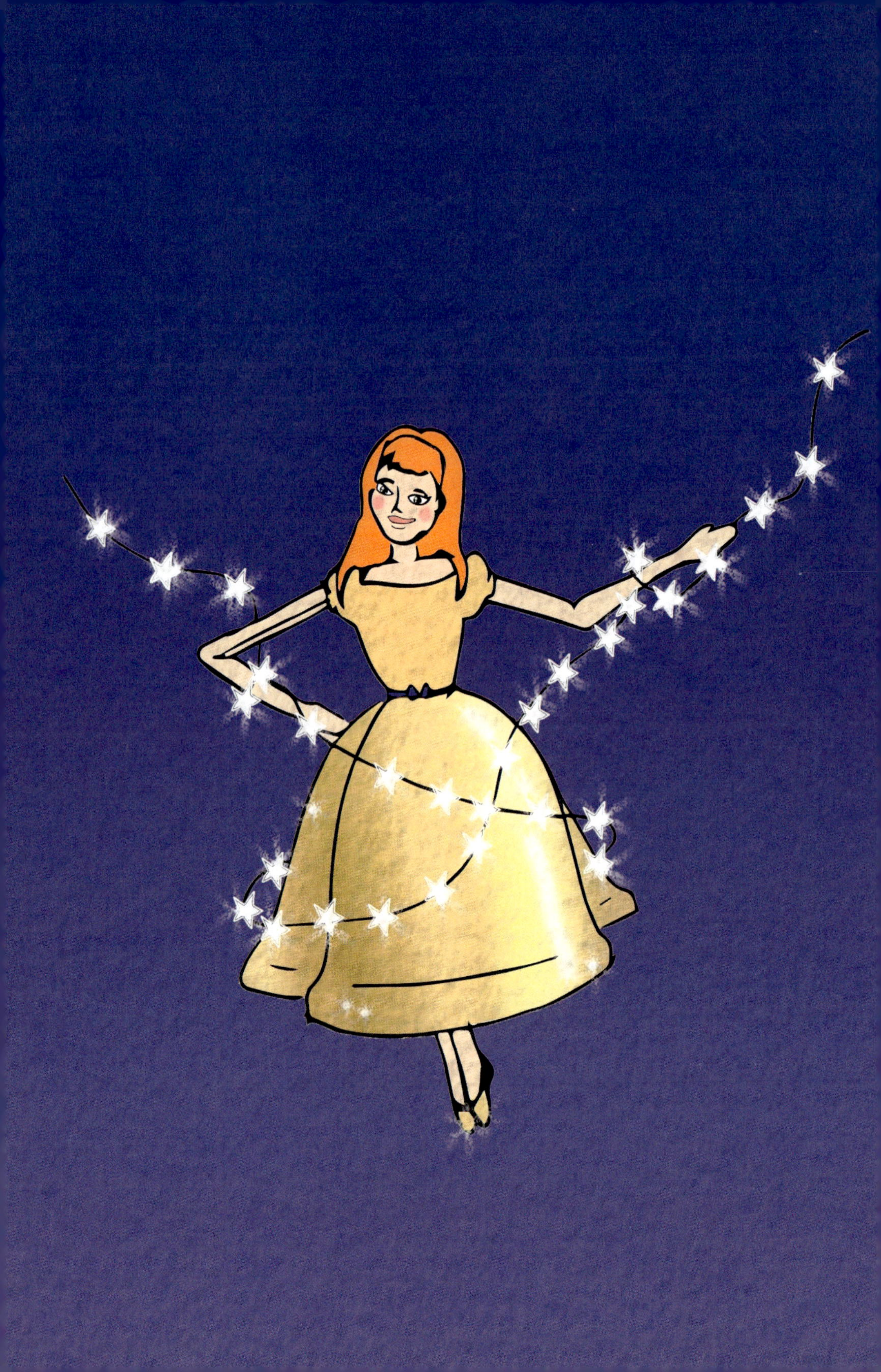

The Bell

Once upon a time there was a little girl whose last name was Bell. She had long, curly red hair that shone just like the sun, olive skin, and big deep black eyes that looked like the reflection of the night on the waves of the ocean. And she was very, very, bright. She could play with numbers and she could count all the leaves on a tree before you even blinked. She could ride a bike with one leg, jump rope 100 times faster than the other girls, eat chocolate for days, and never complain about anything.

Her name was Ginger Bell, and she always liked to dress in white dresses. She liked to draw, dance, and swim. She liked to ride horses, climb trees, and hang upside down. Ginger loved the circus and always dreamed of doing things the trapeze artists did. She saw herself flying amongst the stars, dancing on the air, going through the loops of fire and walking on water. Ginger wasn't afraid of animals either. She shared her cookies and her songs with her friends at school. But Ginger was only one foot tall and her friends often made fun of her. They called her ding-dong and tinkle, tinkle. They usually ate her cookies and took her songs but they always made fun of her.

So, Ginger often came home crying and didn't know what she did wrong. Her mother and father couldn't help her. They told her that she was very special and she had so many gifts. What did it matter if she was one foot tall.

Soon people began to step on her because they said they didn't see her. Then they started calling her Jingle Bells rather than Ginger.

So Ginger didn't know why this was happening-why her friends started going out with boys and turned their backs on her, when she used to make them laugh all the time. She didn't know what happened to their teacher who always had headaches and didn't have time for explanations. She didn't understand why her mother and father didn't have answers to anything, except tell her to eat her dinner and not let their behavior bother her so much. But Ginger was miserable.

So one night Ginger sat by the window crying to the stars about her predicament. Eventually she fell asleep.

A dream came to her that she was floating on a huge green and reddish leaf on a river that was flowing downstream. Soon she saw a beautiful waterfall ahead and the big leaf slid down, so gently with her on top. Without hurting her river had brought her beneath the waterfall. Not only she felt the freshness of the water, this river was alive and it talked to her.

"What is it that you wish from me?" the river inquired.

"Nothing except to be tall! I am to be so tall that I could walk amongst other people?"

"It will be done," the river said.

Suddenly she started to grow taller, and taller, and taller. She had forgotten to tell the river how tall she wanted to be. She grew so tall that her head reached the sky and started burning from the sun.

"What do you want from me?" the sun inquired.

Not being able to stand the heat, Ginger replied, "Nothing. Just to go back to the way I was."

"All right," replied the sun. "It will be done."

So now Ginger started shrinking, but she had forgotten to tell the sun how much she wanted to shrink, so that she almost vanished. But something happened when she shrank almost to a size of a teardrop. A star reached out and saved her from disappearing. Then a snowflake froze her into a tear. Then the stars gathered around her and created a bell around her and she became that bell and began to ring.

Ding-dong, ding-dong, ding-dong, Ginger sang her songs. And because she was a magical bell she floated in the air until she found her home. That night she went to all her friends and sang to them over their heads. Then she floated home, became a little girl again, and went to sleep.

The next day everyone in school was speaking about the floating bell that had visited them the night before. Ginger said that perhaps it was all in their dreams. But they just laughed at her.

So the next night Ginger went by the window and called her stars and asked them if they could make her a bell again. The stars did and she started going to her friends and singing her songs again.

Again everyone was talking about the singing bell the next day, except Ginger who knew the truth.

Ginger started to enjoy her secret of turning into a small bell and floating free. Now she wasn't lonely anymore because she could visit the stars and play with them. She could decorate a tree, or hang on a door, or on a dog's neck. She could send bees away from baby carriages, or she could ring the school bell. She could do so many things no one else could do.

As she was truly enjoying becoming a bell and seeing what people thought, she forgot to see what was really happening around her.

One day all her friends decided to throw a net around the bell when it appeared. So that night when the bell appeared, they threw a net over it and caught it.

"Now you are going to do what we ask you to do," some of the boys said, and they carried the bell everywhere. But the bell refused to make any sounds. Ginger became frightened because if they never let her go, how could she turn back into herself again? What would her parents say when they discovered that she was missing, and what would happen if they found out that she had become a bell. She had all these questions.

The whole school was excited that they had caught the bell. No one else had such a magical floating bell. And as they were pushing to touch the bell, grab the bell, share the bell, one of the little boys pulled it so roughly that the bell fell and broke to pieces.

At that moment Ginger came out of the bell and became her old self. Everyone was speechless. No one knew how Ginger had entered the bell. But suddenly, at that moment, the whole school noticed Ginger for the first time.

Suddenly they all knew that she was very special- that she had the gift of shape shifting.

Then, one by one all the friends who had avoided her apologized to her for not having been able to see how special she was.

Ginger was happy that her friends had come back band because she had learned so much, she was no longer angry if they made fun of her. She knew that she would continue making songs and she would always talk to the stars and hope that her magic bell would return.

She bent and picked up all the broken pieces of the bell and went home. Then she glued the bell back, piece by piece, and put it on the windowsill. That night in her dream, she saw her bell floating away to the stars and she heard all her songs.

The next day, when she woke up, she didn't find her bell on the windowsill. It remains a great secret where her bell went when it vanished, but Ginger still writes songs when her bell visits her in her dreams.

People say that they see her sometimes, walking inside the bell, but it's only their imagination.

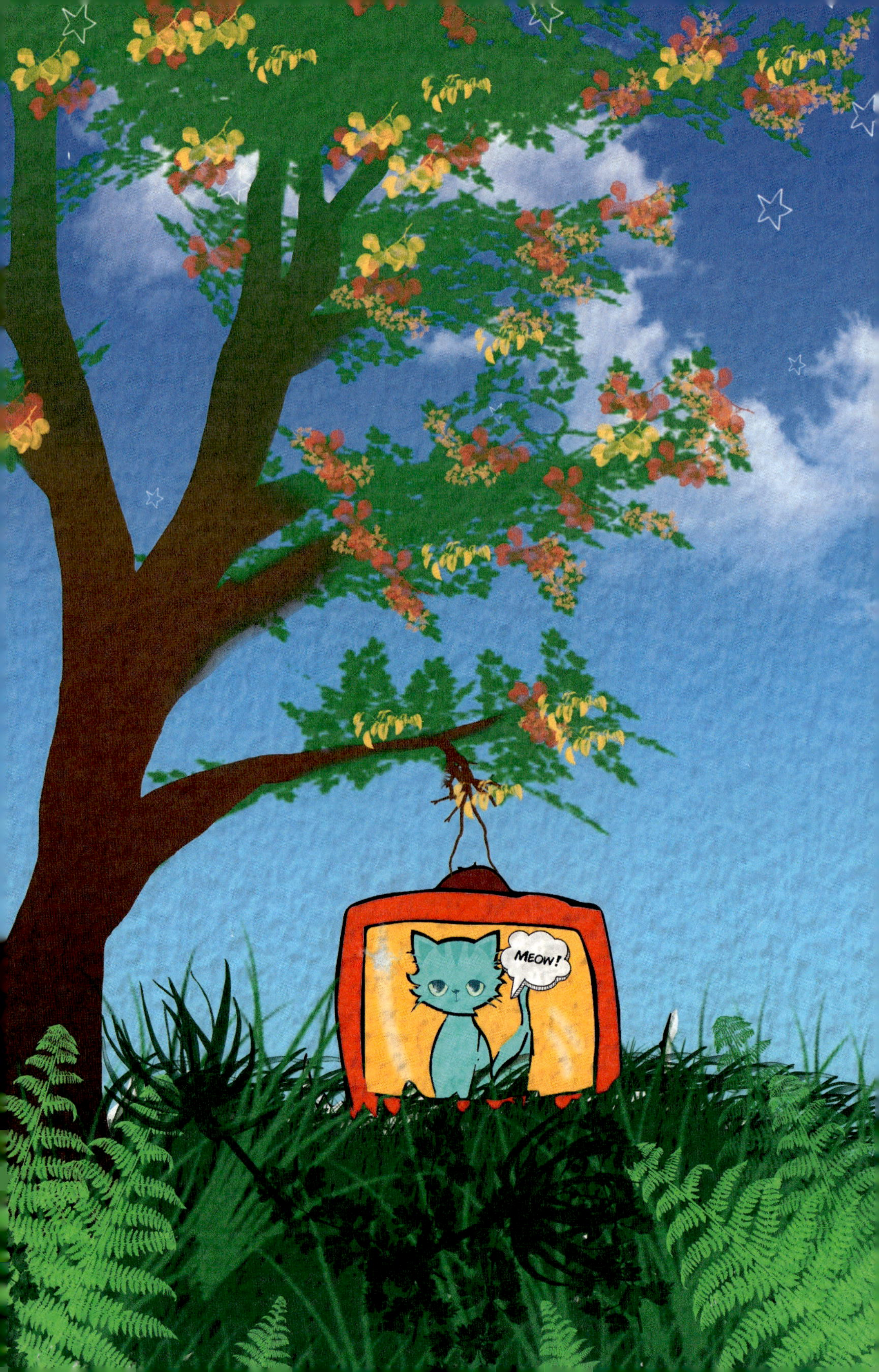
MEOW!

The Tree

Vanessa and William were twins, and they were the only children who had a cat that talked. No one believed them, not even their parents that their cat Misty talked.

Every day, when Vanessa and William's parents went to work, Misty started to talk and all she said was:

"Plant a seed of love and you will get a tree. Plant a tree of love and you will get a seed." That's all Misty ever said and nothing else.

So one day Vanessa said to William "Why don't we listen to Misty and plant a seed of love in our garden?"

"But where are we going to find a seed of love?" William asked.

"I don't know," said Vanessa. "Let's ask Misty."

The two of them asked Misty where they could find a seed of love and Misty just laughed and giggled, moving her tail back and forth between them, pointing towards the tip of their heart.

Each morning Vanessa and William went to their garden and said to the earth " If we plant the seeds of love from our hearts, will you please take them?"

Then they went inside very excited, dreaming about how their seeds of love would grow and how no one would have a garden like theirs filled with most beautiful flowers. People would come to see the flowers and they would know that they grew from seeds of love. They would want to pick them, but they would have to ask Vanessa and William first.

They also told Misty not to tell anyone else about the seeds of love because everyone would laugh. So the three of them had a secret and every morning they ran to the window to see if there were any flowers or a tree in the garden. They were disappointed when each morning they found nothing growing in their garden, but they were determined, and each morning they went out to plant more seeds of their love.

So day after day after day, for one thousand and one days, in rows they planted the seeds of love, yet nothing grew in their garden. And then they lost their faith in the seed of love. They never told anyone again that their cat Misty spoke. They began to doubt if any of that was true at all.

Then the winter came, on Christmas Day, when nothing grows in the cold and everything was covered with snow, Vanessa and William heard their mother scream.

"Oh, my God! Oh my God, where did this come from?" She cried.

Vanessa and William ran to the window and they couldn't believe their eyes. In the garden where they had planted the seeds of love had grown a huge, tall tree with magic silver and crystal leaves in the shape of the hearts. The tree was as white as snow.

Vanessa and William jumped of joy and they squeezed their cat and kissed her for knowing and they knew that she had been right all along. At last the seeds of love had grown in their backyard.

It was a secret how the tree grew there, because no one believed that the cat was the only one who knew how it all came about. People came to visit the tree from all over the country, and they touched it and somehow it was a real tree. When children stood under the tree to play, the branches gave each child a leaf as a gift. The children were asked to suck the leaf and a sweet, milky, honey filled their mouths. The tree, however, remained crystal-silver and lasted forever. The secret was that when anyone was upset at anything at all, they needed to do was suck a leaf and they would forget what they were angry about.

So more and more people came to their garden and Vanessa and William made so many friends. Each morning they planted more seeds of love around the tree and they always talked to the tree. The tree loved Vanessa and William and it gave them so many gifts. They kept the rest a secret, because they were afraid that everyone would want too much from the tree.

But as more and more people came to visit the tree, they were not satisfied with just one leaf. They wanted more leaves. Soon they started to want branches and they started reaching up and breaking off the tree.

Vanessa and William could not help the tree. They cried and asked their parents to help them, but no one could stop the people who started coming to their garden at night and taking everything they could from the tree.

Little by little the tree started losing its leaves and soon there were just a few bare branches left.

"Why do people do this?" Vanessa cried to her mother, who didn't really know the answer.

Then one day when they awoke the tree of love was gone. Where the tree had stood, now the place was empty. They couldn't believe their eyes and didn't know what had happened.

Vanessa and William were alone again and they asked Misty what had happened. All Misty said was, " Plant a seed of love and you will get a tree. Plant a tree of love and you will get a seed." Misty said nothing else.

Soon enough a lady from a television station heard that Vanessa and William had a cat who could talk. She sent someone out to ask them and asked them if they would like their cat to be on TV.

So that's how Misty ended up on TV appearing on talk shows and saying the only thing she knew:" Plant a seed of love and you will get a tree. Plant a tree of love and you will get a seed." After all, Misty said nothing else.

When they saw Misty on TV, many children started to plant their seeds of love in their gardens. Newspapers wrote about the magic tree of love that once grew in Vanessa and William's garden and they printed pictures of them near the tree.

And even though, no one knows when the tree of love will come back, again, but Misty is sure that it will be any day now.

The Horse

Once there was this boy who couldn't sit still for a moment. His name was Reggio, and he had charcoal black eyes like the forest in the night, black curly hair, and bronze colored skin. He had freckles on his nose and big feet.

Reggio liked to jump all over the house-from the couch on top of the dresser, from the bathtub to the ceiling, from the top of the stairs to the ground, and he liked to pretend that he was flying. He climbed trees and hung upside down for hours. He stood on his head, so he could see the world the way he wanted, and he didn't like to eat vegetables. He drove his mother crazy when he would fall asleep under the bed and no one could find him.

The kids at school called him a bullet because he ran fast and never stopped. He didn't have many friends because no one was as fast as he was and no one else did the things he did.

One day he was running home a different way than usual. When he crossed the lake on an old boat, in the park he saw from a distance a little girl, all dressed in white, talking to a black horse.

The horse was big and shiny and was carefully listening to the girl in white. She was trying to ride

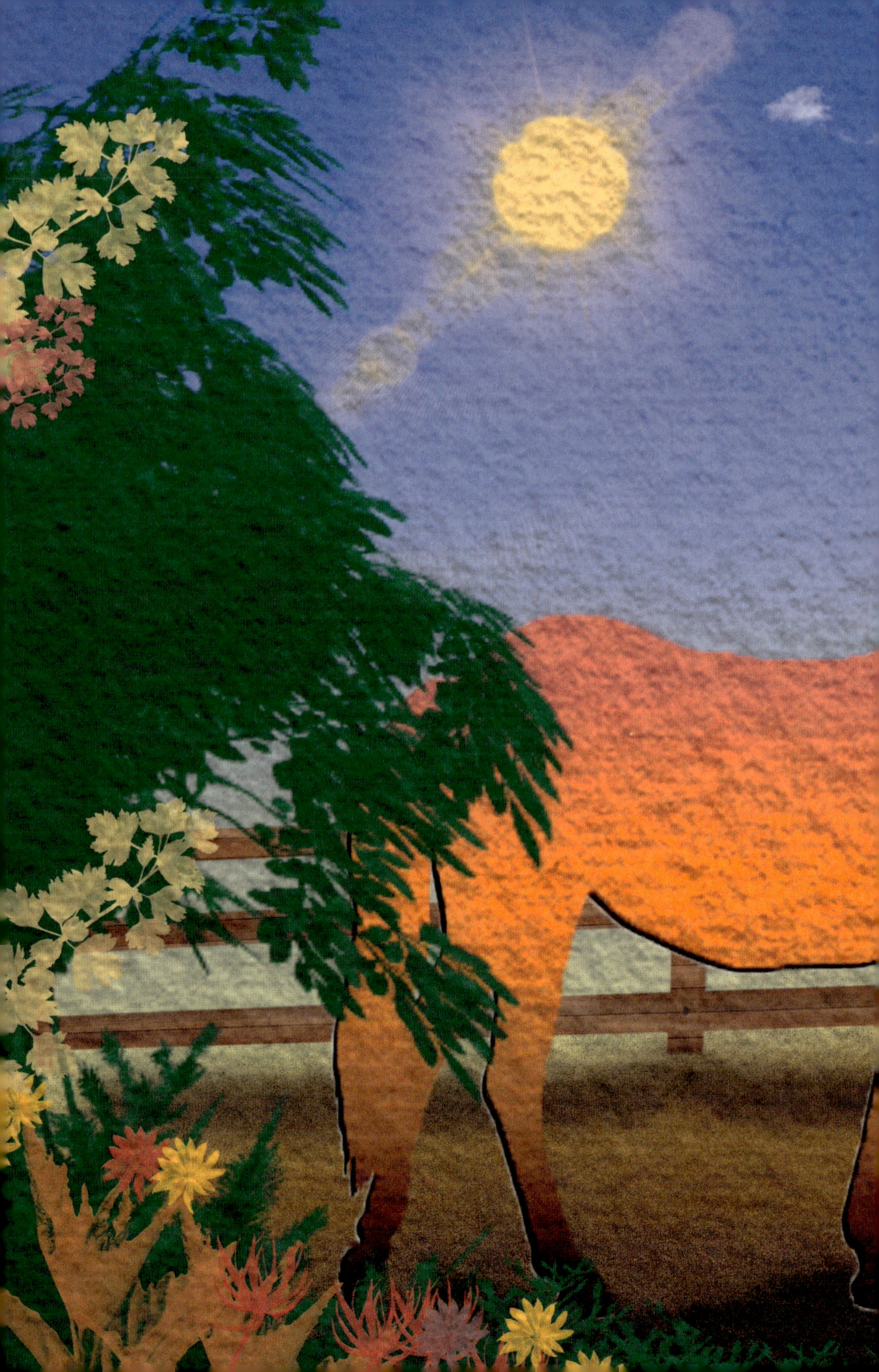

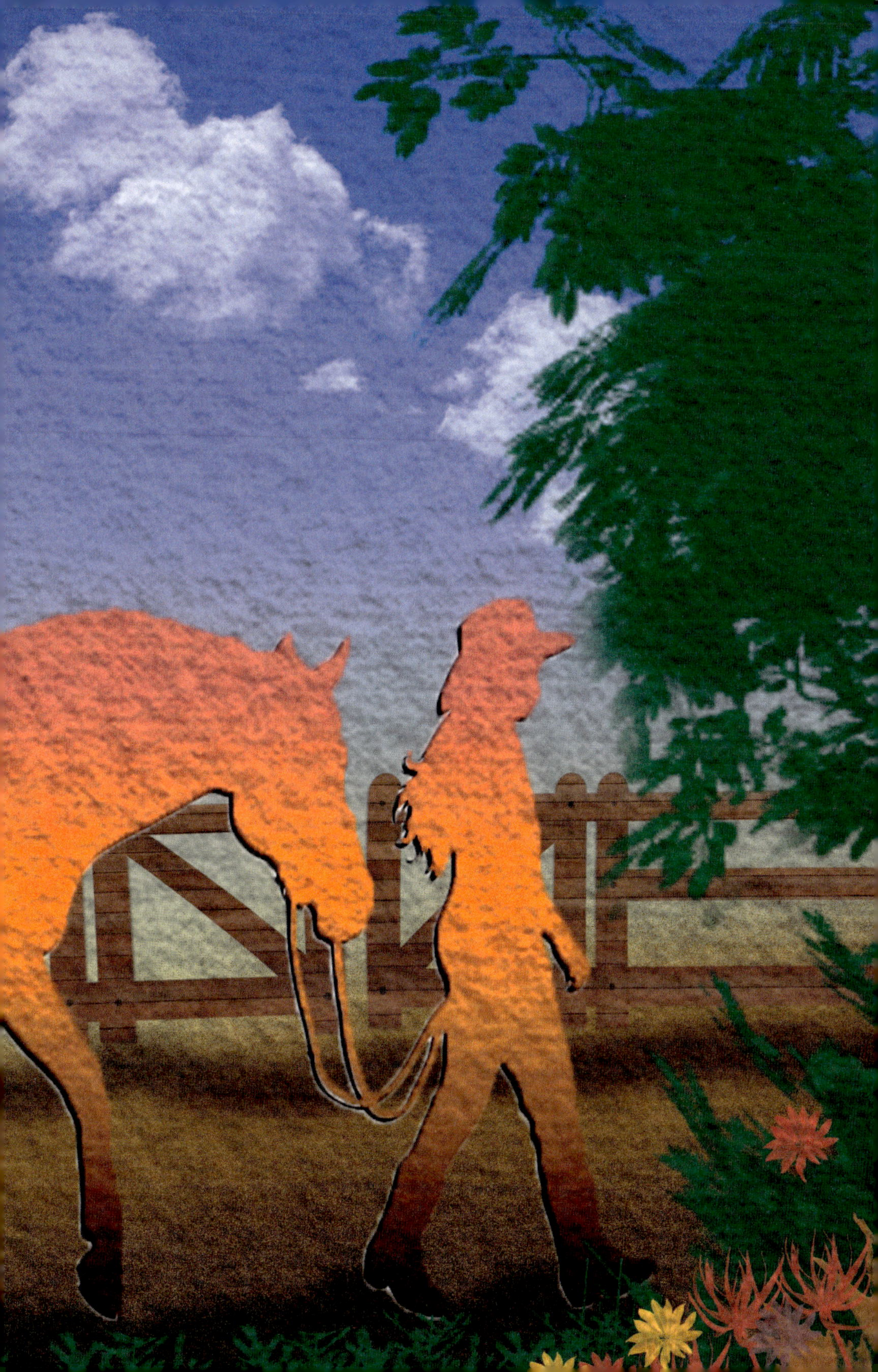

the horse, but she was too short and couldn't jump onto the saddle.

Reggio loved the horse. He had never had a horse and for a moment he started dreaming. "Imagine if I had that horse how fast I could ride across the mountains and, I could race. I could fly away and no one would ever be able to stop me."

All of a sudden, he had the feeling that he was growing taller and taller and that he could reach for the horse from where he was standing. He and his horse could be friends and no one could take this away.

The horse, as if it sensed something, looked towards Reggio and began running wild. The girl tried to stop him, but she couldn't, so she started to cry.

Reggio used this moment to show her how fast he was. He ran over the hills by the lake and began running after the horse, then he jumped his triple jump and landed on the horse, that was really wild. The girl couldn't believe her eyes. How could a little boy jump like that onto the back of a galloping horse?

Reggio loved riding the horse, but he finally had to get off and give the little girl her horse back.

"My name is Adriane," she said. "How can you jump like that?"

"I have been jumping since I was a baby, he said. "My name is Reggio."

So from that day on Adriane and Reggio met every afternoon and rode the horse. He taught her how to jump, and how to run, and how to jump onto saddle.

They brought sweet apples and pears for the horse. One day they baked a cake and named the horse Wind and became best friends forever.

Adriane told Reggio about her life in a big mansion and about her loneliness. She had no brothers or sisters and her parents traveled a lot. She usually spent her time with her nanny and her tutors. The only time she was allowed to be alone and free was with her horse in the park, until their chauffeur picked her up.

Reggio told her about his small apartment; his parents who loved to cook and sometimes forgot about him. He told her how once while he was jumping his sock fell off and fell into his Mom's soup pot. He was afraid to tell her what happened so they all ate the soup. Reggio told Adriane that his mother told him the most wonderful stories, and his father took him fishing, but he could never catch a fish. So Reggio would dive and put a fish on his father's hook.

The both of them laughed, shared stories, played, and shared everything with Wind.

Wind was never happier before. He loved Adriane and had been there for her since she was born. He taught her about riding, tall trees, rivers, and clouds. He taught her to love and the two of them shared the same loneliness. Adriane's father had bought Wind when he was very little and he had grown up behind Adriane's home.

One day Wind heard Adriane's father and mother talking about moving. They had sold the house and were going to go away. This news saddened Wind, who didn't know how to take it.

"How is my Adriane going to take this?" he thought. " She has finally found a friend and they are going to take her away from him. Wind couldn't let this happen. He would never be apart from Adriane.

That night he ran away from the mansion. He ran through the park, crossed the lake, and disappeared into the mountains.

When Adriane didn't find her horse in the morning, she began to cry hysterically. No one could make her feel better. Everyone in her household was searching for Wind, but no trace of him could be found.

Reggio went by the lake every day, but when Adriane and Wind didn't come the whole week, he decided to go to her mansion.

When he got there, they told him that Adriane was lying sick in bed. He demanded to see her and, when they told him that he couldn't, he climbed a tree and jumped inside her room through the open window.

Adriane was very sick with longing for Wind. She couldn't imagine her life without him. The place they were going in the city. There was no stable there for Wind. Her father had promised her many other things, but she had no desire to go, so she became sick and refused to get out of bed.

Reggio promised to find Wind and bring him back to her. That night he went toward the mountains, climbing trees, and calling Wind by his name.

For days and nights, he walked through the mountains until he came down on the other side, by the sea. Then Reggio sat on the beach and, being very tired then Reggio fell asleep.

Suddenly in the middle of his sleep he felt someone sniffing his hair. He opened his eyes and saw Wind, over him. He jumped standing for joy and hugged him.

"Adriane has been sick since you ran away," he said to the Wind. "You have to help her. You have to come back."

But Wind neighed as if to say, "But if I come back they will sell me, and then I will never be free again."

Reggio and Wind played all day together and somehow by nightfall Reggio convinced Wind to go back. He rode the horse all the way to Adriane's house.

When they came under Adriane's window, Reggio jumped again on the tree and into her room. He woke her up and took her with him climbing down the tree and onto the back of Wind. Adriane's face was shining from joy. She hugged and kissed Wind and told him that she would never let him go. Then Wind took off.

Wind was running with both children on his back. He passed the park, the lake, and disappeared into the mountains. When he crossed the mountains, he brought them to the other side.

Adriane had never seen such a blue sea, and the sun and the moon met there at the end of the sea. The clouds that covered them had a golden glow, and the grass was a lush green. She had never seen caves with long crystal walls, or waterfalls that sounded like bells.

This was unlike anything she had ever known. She and Reggio and Wind swam in the blue waves and built a fire, and danced, and sang. They were so happy.

However, Adriane and Reggio's parents were very concerned about their children, so they invited all the people in the village to search for them. They searched everywhere, but couldn't find them.

You see it remains a secret where the three of them went when they disappeared? when the people arrived at the beach, they couldn't find the children or the horse.

Days passed and the parents went home and cried for their children and missed them very much. Adriane's father prayed on his knees that he would not sell the manssion and move away, if only Adriane returned.

Then one day, early in the morning, when the sun was glowing and its brilliant rays were shining over the lake, Wind with the two children on his back, slowly rode toward the house.

Everyone was so happy to see the children and the horse.

No one ever asked them where they had been, and the next day they threw a big party in their backyard. Adriane got to know some of the other children and everyone had a ride on Wind. Of course Reggio was a star for finding Adriane.

That's how Reggio and Adriane stayed in the village and Wind got to watch them grow up playing together.

Wind kept the secret to himself about life on the other side of the mountain because the children couldn't remember how they got there.

The Grasshopper

There once was a shy boy named Tim who wore thick glasses. His friends at school called him stupid because he stuttered. But Tim wasn't stupid at all, he was quiet and avoided talking when he didn't have to.

Many of his friends had no patience with him, so they always invited him to things that he didn't like to do. And when he refused them, they called him heartless and turned their backs on him. After school Tim usually walked home alone through the park and thought about everything. On his way home he walked across town and sat by the river and watched the sunset over the river.

One day he met this grasshopper that jumped on his knees.

"Why are you looking so sad?" asked the grasshopper.

Tim jumped in surprise before he could even answer. He didn't know that grasshoppers could talk. After a while he told the grasshopper that he missed his friends and that he was very lonely.

"Are your friends saying that you don't have a heart?" the grasshopper continued.

"Yes," said Tim.

The grasshopper thought and thought, then decided

to help him get his friends back.

"Look," he said, "I have a plan." And he whispered his plan in Tim's ear.

Tim rolled with laughter, and then he took the grasshopper with him to his home.

Tim's father was a truck driver. He usually was on the road for a whole month, and when came back, he would always be sleeping, because he was tired.

When Tim wanted to spend some time with his father, he always said, "Tomorrow."

Tim's mother worked long hours in the chocolate factory, and when she came home, she was tired too. But at least she brought him all kinds of chocolates from work.

Tim's parents didn't even notice that Tim had a guest at home: the grasshopper. Everything went the usual way. They ate dinner, and everyone told his or her side of the story of what happened all day long, until they went to their rooms.

This time Tim was so happy to show the grasshopper his books, his basketball, and his television. The grasshopper had never seen a television, so he jumped right on the screen and was staring at the moving pictures.

The grasshopper was excited because he discovered a world he didn't know.

The next day Tim took the grasshopper with him to school. Right in the middle of class, the grasshopper jumped from Tim's pocket into a boy's ear.

The boy jumped and screamed not knowing what

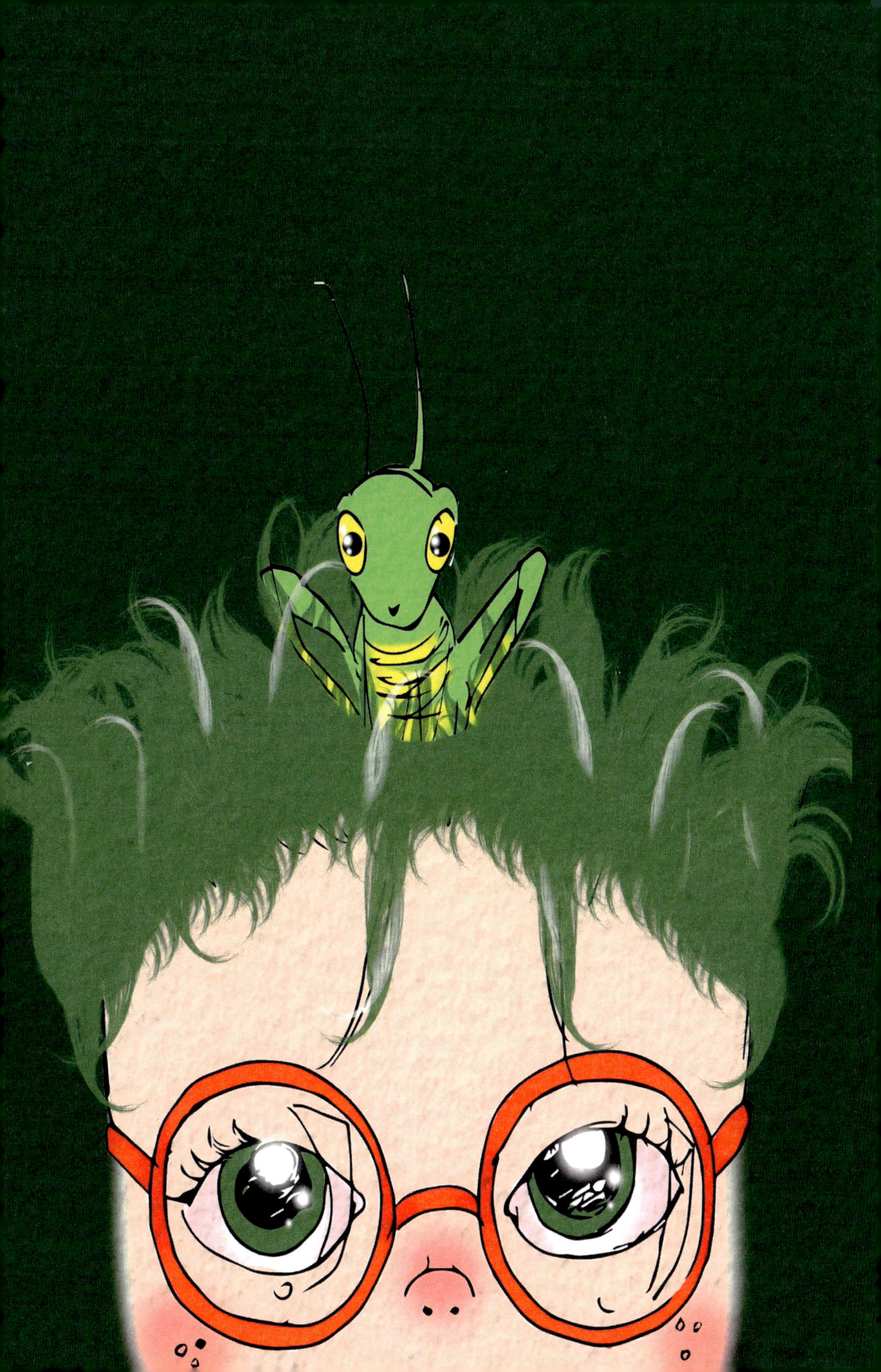

was moving inside his ear.

"Ah! Ah! Ah!" the boy screamed.

The teacher didn't understand what was wrong. Everyone panicked and the class was interrupted.

Tim understood immediately what was happening. He came close to the boy, shook his head, then he placed his palm on his ear, and everything stopped. No one had seen the grasshopper.

The class continued, and everyone looked at Tim wondering how he calmed the boy.

This game didn't end that day. Every day the grasshopper jumped inside someone else's ear and every day was the same thing. No one knew how to calm down that person, except for Tim.

Soon it became a big deal. The newspaper wrote about what was happening, the radio and television reported on the events. The teachers gathered and discussed what it could be that makes children jump, scream, and shake like that.

So they invited Tim to a meeting and asked him what he did that everything stopped when he touched them. Since Tim stuttered so hard, they didn't understand a word he said and they were disappointed.

Then a doctor and priest came and it became a really big thing.

"Listen," Tim said to the grasshopper, "we'd better stop this game. It's getting out of hand."

But the grasshopper wasn't going to give up his new game so easily. He was helping his friend get all this attention and becoming the center of attention. He was having so much fun tickling people when he jumped in their ears.

The following day at school, although the grasshopper had promised Tim that he wouldn't do it, he jumped into a girl's ear and did it again.

Tim was really hurt because he had asked his little green friend to stop it. So he stood and took him away again.

This time though everyone thought that Tim was a sweetheart, but they were determined to find the truth about his secret.

The teacher followed Tim home, climbed up on the window, and saw Tim talking to the grasshopper.

When Tim came to school the next day, everyone was waiting for him in the classroom: the dean, all the teachers, his friends, and everyone else from town. They accused him of having deliberately brought the grasshopper to school. They asked him to give them the grasshopper and to stay a week away from school as a punishment.

The grasshopper saw that he had gotten Tim in a lot of trouble and asked Tim to give him to them. But Tim knew that they would place the grasshopper in a glass jar and keep him there to show everyone what he had done.

He ran out of the classroom without turning his head or giving up his grasshopper. He then came to his secret place by the river where he had found the grasshopper in the first place and set him free.

"It was fun," the grasshopper said. "At least they couldn't do anything about me, but you could."

Tim had tears in his eyes when he said goodbye to his friend.

"Will I see you again?" he asked.

"I will surprise you one day," the grasshopper said. "Just when you don't expect it."

After a week Tim went back to school. This time he had more friends than before because they wanted to know where he got that grasshopper. Slowly Tim began telling them all kinds of stories, and little by little he forgot to stutter.

Two years passed. Tim was doing well in school and he had a lot of friends, because his stories about the grasshopper had grown so big that everyone loved them and wanted to hear them.

One night while he was asleep, he felt that something was moving inside his ear. He jumped out of bed and shook his head, but nothing came out. He was shaking and jumping and screaming, but nothing came out. His mother and father came in, but they couldn't help. Then he remembered his friend the grasshopper and asked him to come out of his ear. But the grasshopper didn't come out.

Tim's mother helped him go to sleep and that night Tim had a dream. The grasshopper had come to visit him and he was telling Tim all kinds of stories.

Since that night Tim has dreamt of the grasshopper

every night and the next day he always writes the story he heard the night before from the grasshopper. Then he tells it to his friends. It was a secret how the grasshopper found his way into Tim's ear and then into Tim's dreams. But since then Tim has grown up and he has become the most famous grasshopper storyteller.

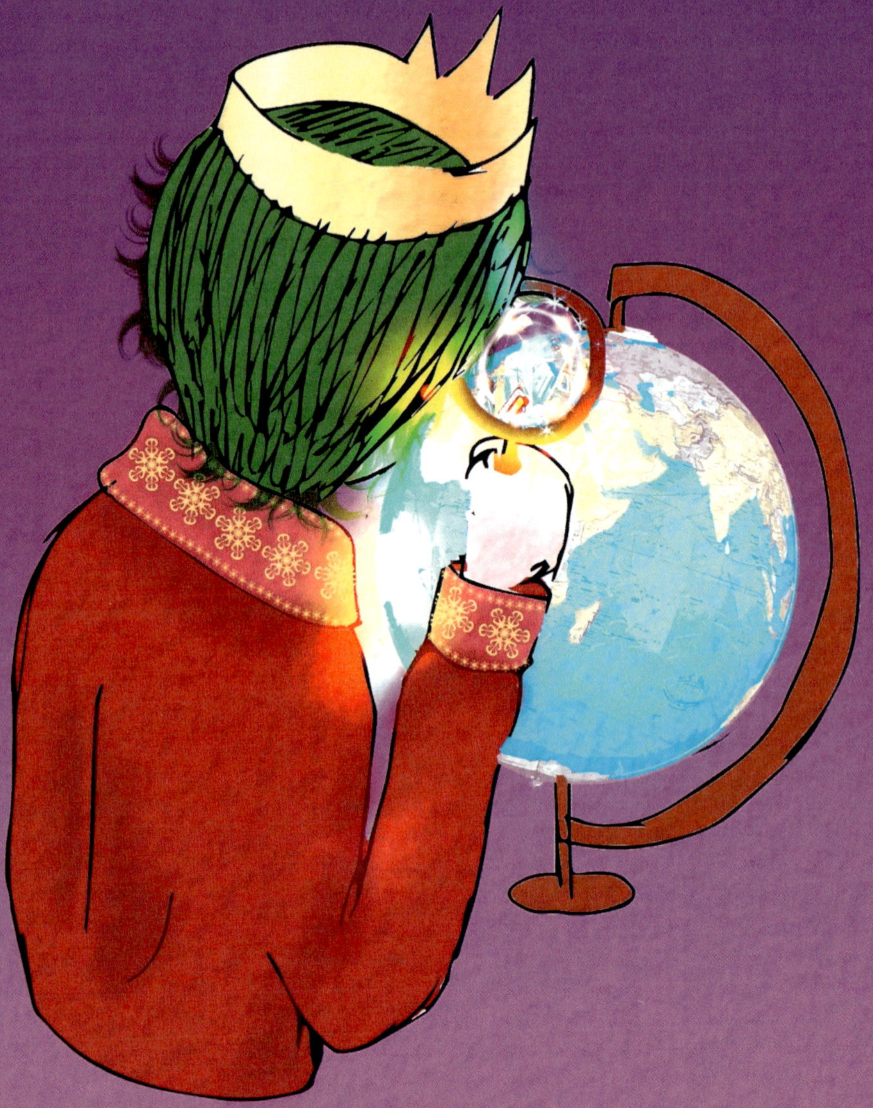

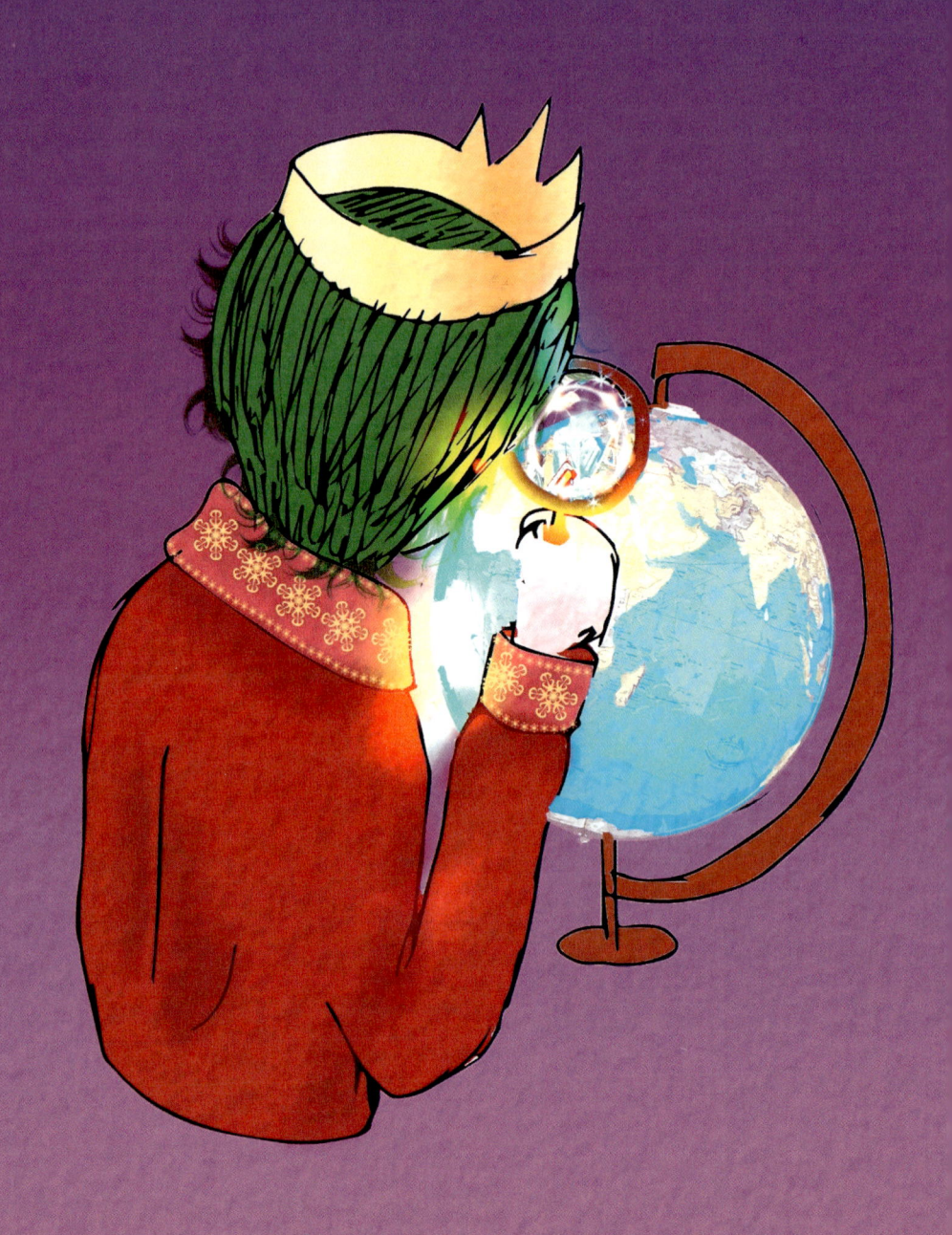

The Truth

Once there was a king named Jordan who lost his way in time. He went from place to place, from time to time, looking for truth, but he couldn't find it.

On his journey he changed so much, since people in different times and places didn't know that he was a king, they treated him like themselves.

Once Jordan ended up selling tobacco for an old man so he could earn his living. He didn't like smoking, but he had no other choice.

"Is this the truth about life?" he asked the old man. "People come and go, and buy and sell, and smoke puff-puff, puff-puff. "

"That's the truth son, " the old man said. "You got that right."

But King Jordan, who had forgotten where he was from, was not satisfied with that answer. To just come and go and buy and sell wasn't enough for him.

"There must be something more to it," he said to himself and continued on his journey.

He ended up much after traveling in a small tavern in a village far away from everyone and everything. Jordan started working in the tavern serving people food and drinks.

He saw how people came and ate and drank, and got drunk, and then left.

After a certain time, he asked the owner: "Is this the truth about life: people come and go, and eat and drink, and get drunk?"

"You got that right," the owner said.

But Jordan didn't like that truth either. There was nothing good or happy or exciting to just come and go, and eat and drink, and get drunk. So he left again, while the people nodded their heads.

"What is he looking for?" they asked.

So he travelled again to some other places and some other times, and he saw how children are born, and how they cry and laugh, and how they grow up.

He discovered the sunset, the sunrise, winds and rains. He discovered blue, restless waters and calm, green ponds. He saw small glittering fish that made light for other fish as they moved. He saw birds flying high in the sky without ever getting tired.

As he continued looking for truth, he found rivers and different lands with spectacular dances, plentiful songs, and musical languages. He also discovered myriads of colors.

So this is how King Jordan ended up being a baker, a babysitter, and a clown in a circus, making everyone laugh except himself. He worked on a ship and on a train and on an airplane. He was a teacher, a doctor, and a priest. He became a father to some child who needed one, and a friend to another.

King Jordan tried everything and yet he couldn't find the truth about life.

One day he ended up in New York, just about in our time. He couldn't understand the tall buildings that rose higher than the sky. Then he saw thousands of stores and thousands of people coming and going and coming and going. Some walked with their heads bent, some walked smiling, some walked smoking, but they all went somewhere. He tried to stop some people and ask them if this was the truth about life, but they ran away from him, afraid to speak to a stranger.

Then King Jordan tried to get a job like he had done in previous times and places, but everywhere he went people just took one look at him and closed their doors.

King Jordan didn't understand what was happening. He looked at himself in the mirror and couldn't find a single thing wrong.

"Wow!" said he to himself. "This couldn't be the truth about life. People are lost, afraid, hiding, and not friendly at all."

He walked for days and nights. He saw boats circling around the city of lights. He saw people sleeping on the streets. He saw others selling hot dogs and pretzels all night long. He saw people drinking. He saw beautiful women with painted faces and colorful dresses walking as fast as men. He saw bookstores, restaurants, and policemen on their horses. He saw everything but birds and fishes and animal friends. When he saw dogs in the leashes, he thought they must be suffering and he tried to free one, but he ended up getting beat up.

He walked and walked and walked and no one gave him anything to eat or drink. No one opened the door to give him him a place to sleep and no one gave him a job.

Then he dragged himself to the river and sat there crying, "This couldn't be the truth about life! What's wrong with me?"

Suddenly he heard a frog saying " Pee-wee, pee-wee, there's nothing wrong with you, King Jordan. You just don't know their language."

King Jordan looked at the frog and couldn't believe his eyes.

"Where did you come from?" he asked.

"I have been living here for centuries," the frog answered.

"Where are other the frogs?" inquired King Jordan.

"I am the only one left," said the frog. "There are no others."

"So how can you live alone?" Jordan asked.

"I am not alone. I have my song pee-wee, pee-wee,"

"What's your song?" King asked.

"It's a secret, pee-wee, pee-wee."

So the King forgot his misery for a moment because he was so happy to meet the only frog in New York City.

"Do you happen to know what the truth about life is?" King Jordan asked.

" Sure I know!" exclaimed the frog.

"You do?" said King Jordan astonished. "You are the

only one out of all the people I've met in my entire life who knows the truth. Could you tell me what it is please?"

"The truth cannot be told," said the frog. "It has to be discovered."

"But I have been so long looking for it and, as of yet, I have not found it. Everywhere I go, every time I find something else. I just cannot figure it out," said King Jordan, feeling absolutely miserable.

"It's magic," said the frog. "Look at me in this little pond; no one knows I even exist. I go in, and out, and then I go in again. When I go in, it's dark, and when I go out, It's light. In and out I sing my song pee-wee, pee-wee. I can tell when it will rain and when the winds will blow. I am happy when I am singing and when I am jumping. Then the leaves fall every autumn as I climb, and I can even float. It's the winter that makes it harder, so I must stay under the ice, but no longer am I frightened, because the spring brings its joys again. I have seen smiling faces when I try to jump. I have seen people jump over me when I step on their toes. So it's magic. It's magic. Just look around and you can see, and hear me pee-wee, pee-wee. " The frog sang.

Suddenly King Jordan, as if waking up from a deep sleep, began to see things clearly. He saw a gentle moon greeting him and, with her lightface she made the tall buildings look like ballerinas. Her reflection floated down the river as if she were dancing and she also danced on the pond and danced with the frog. Then she touched every tree and leaf and blade ofgrass and the faces of all who looked at her glowed.

The truth was that life wasn't just about coming and going and buying and selling and sinking and falling. It was about flying and diving, walking and talking, singing and dancing, breathing and catching. Life was about seeing the colors, smelling the flowers, taking showers on the rainy days. It was about laughing and crying, dreaming and hiding, and facing it all. It was only a moment of being in time.

He saw long streets stretching like endless colorful shoestrings and people sliding up and down with happy faces.

"They are probably looking for the truth too," the King thought.

And then he understood that if he wanted to stay here he would have to change, and learn their language and dress like them, walk and dance like them.

He thought for a while and realized that he missed his home and his family and his friends that he had forgotten on his long search for the truth.

"I have changed enough," he said to the frog.

"I am very grateful to you for showing me the way to the truth," King Jordan said. "I must go back."

So he said goodbye to the frog and started his journey back in time. This time he knew the way and he travelled there fairly easily. Whatever he saw and whatever he became, he enjoyed very much and never asked anyone if that was the truth about life.

When he finally came home, everyone was waiting for him. They celebrated his return for days and nights. They ate and drank, and danced, and asked King Jordan to tell them stories about his journey.

So the king sat under a tree as people came to listen, and he told them stories about times and places and people and things he had seen and what he had learned about life.

He told them about everything except his little secret that he learned the truth from a frog. And that's how it came to be that no one knows that some frogs can actually tell the truth about life with their little pee-wee song. But it's a secret where all those frogs have disappeared to, so now no one can find a wise King or a magical frog anymore. It's a secret.

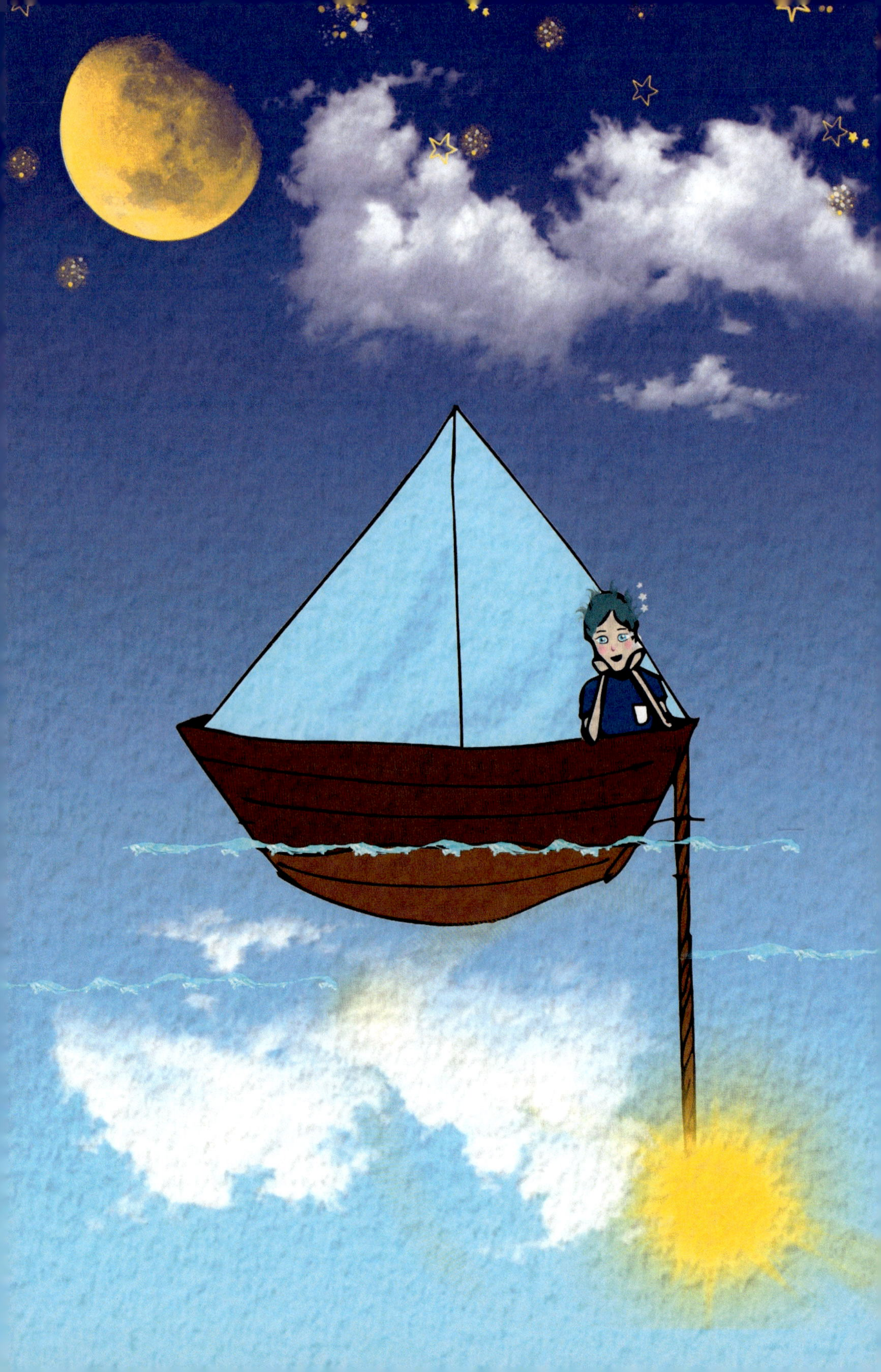

The Secret

One day a little boy named Martin heard on the radio that whoever found a buried secret would win a trip on a ship to all the lands of the world, and enough money to afford everything one could ever buy.

"Aha," Martin thought, "I will find the secret." But he didn't know what the secret was. If he didn't know what it was, how could he find it? This became a big problem for him now.

That night he had a dream that he was walking on a long rope tied from one end of the sky to the other. Beneath him was the sea and above him, the blue sky. As he walked, trying not to fall, he saw two hands made of light pick him up. He didn't know whose hands they were, but somehow he wasn't scared. Then he saw that the hands were carrying him beyond the rainbow, through lovely pink and purple clouds, over the silver green forests and blue waterfalls, and brought him down in the middle of a valley.

Then the hands placed him there and disappeared. Suddenly, all the animals from the animal kingdom came out. They, too, were made of light and greeted him. Martin still wasn't afraid.

"What is it that you are looking for? Why are you

here?" the lion asked.

"Well, I want to be the one who discovers the secret. Then I get to go around the world on a ship," Martin replied.

The animals gathered together and started to talk amongst themselves.

"We can't give you the secret about the secret," the lion continued, "but we can help you to understand the way to go about it."

Then the lion gave Martin the long rope on which he had walked and said to him, "Use this when you need it." Afterwards they left him one by one.

This time the moon picked him up and carried him through the night. The moon showed Martin how his city looks at night when everyone is asleep.

He could see his friends' homes and what they had on the windows. He saw that there was no secret for the moon, because she saw everything and everyone.

The moon gently put him on his bed and went back to the sky.

As the days passed, he heard on the radio that people were getting very excited looking for the secret. Everyday someone would come up with something he or she found and they would announce on the radio. One day someone found a red shoe, but that wasn't a secret. There were things like a bucket filled with coins, boxes of rings and earrings. There was even a doll without a hand! There was a pipe, a book, a pot, a horn, an upside down ship, etc. All kinds of things were announced on the radio, but they were not secrets and the prize was not awarded to anyone.

Each day, when Martin heard that the secret still had not been found, he had hope that he would find the secret, and the prize would be given to him.

After one thousand, one hundred and one nights, Martin had another dream. This time he was riding a white stallion down the greenest of valleys. As he was riding he could reach the top of the forest trees, he could touch the sun and the moon and he could grasp the stars.

As he was riding, the stars greeted him and fell on his shoulders wanting to be his friends. The moon gave him her light and kissed him on his lips, and the sun gave him his fire. When he came to the sea, he saw his face reflected on the water and heard a voice saying, "The secret is, the secret is, that I am the water… That I, the water, gave you the color of your eyes." Then the voice disappeared.

Martin woke up and went by the sea. He knew that this was the help that his animal friends had talked about. When he got to the beach, he noticed a long rope lying on the sand, slowly vanishing somewhere deep inside the sea. He dove inside the waters, not knowing what he was looking for.

The sea then wrapped the rope around Martin's waist and pulled him down to the bottom. Suddenly he couldn't believe his eyes. There at the bottom of the sea, he saw a whole new world. He saw scintillating fish talking to each other. He saw mermaids dancing and singing. He saw crystal stairs, and ships floating. The sea stars shone through the water, and the flowers blossomed at the bottom of the sea just the same as as they do on land. He discovered boxes filled with glittering rocks of all different colors. He saw someone in the distance drawing, and someone else swimming, and someone else swinging on the rope. But he knew that whatever he saw wasn't the secret.

Then the rope pulled him gently toward an empty cave. He went inside the cave and moved slowly without fear, but found nothing. Suddenly, from a distance two big eyes appeared before him. The eyes were huge; then two big hands grabbed him. This time he began to tremble. "Maybe this is a monster and he's going to eat me, " he thought, but no such thing happened. Then he heard a voice talking to him.

"I hear that you are still looking for the secret?"

"I am," Martin replied.

"You don't like to give up, do you?"

"No, I don't ever give up," Martin said.

Then the voice whispered something in Martin's ear and the hands let him go.

The rope pulled Martin right back onto the beach and when he turned around the rope had disappeared. He then went home with a smiling face and went to sleep.

The next day when Martin woke up he thought a lot about what had happened to him the night before at the bottom of the sea, but he decided not to tell anyone about it.

But when his mother saw him at breakfast she screamed.

"Oh my god!"

"I can't believe it, what happened to you?" yelled Martin's mother.

"What?" Martin asked, surprised.

"Your eyes have turned blue that's what! You never had blue eyes before," she cried.

Martin looked in the mirror and there he was with the bluest eyes he had ever seen. Actually they were the same color as the depths of the sea.

" No, I've always had blue eyes," he lied to his mother. "You probably didn't notice them." But he hid the secret about the sea. He was pretty sure that he had gotten the bluest color eyes from down there, at the bottom of the sea.

Everyone at school was also very surprised at the sudden change of color of Martin's eyes. Martin didn't want to bring much attention to himself, so he wore glasses, and from that day on, no one else bothered him.

Then, when the radio station announced that no one had found the buried secret, they admitted that this was only a joke the announcer had played to make the program more interesting, that they knew that there was no such thing as the buried secret. When Martin heard this, he went straight to the radio station and demanded to speak on the air.

"I found the secret," Martin said. "And it's not a thing. It's not a box, or a shoe, or a doll, or a coin. It's not made of matter." Then he told his story of how he ended up at the bottom of the sea because he had a dream, and how a voice whispered in his ear what the secret was.

And this is what Martin said, "It's a song that has been buried under the sea for millions and millions of years."

He then sang the song, which was all about LOVE.

Then he ended up by saying, "now you know the secret, and I give you all the secret of love that I brought from the bottom of the sea. "

To prove the magic of love and that the secret was true, he told them about the change of color in his eyes.

That is how Martin won the prize and ended up travelling on a ship around the world. Wherever he went, he sang his song of love and people loved it and presented him with the most beautiful gifts.

Since then, Martin has been singing his song of love, so it's no longer a secret. The song goes something like this:

Love is a miracle, a miracle, a miracle.
Love is the smile on your face.
Love blossoms forth in flowers
It's the gleam in your eyes when you're in an embrace.
Love is wonder, a wonder, a wonder.
Love is the blue of the seas.
And when it rains in the evening,
It's love that trickles down swaying the leaves.
Love is the sweet song, that sweet song once buried,
And, sung now by every soul.
Love grows as berries on bushes.

It's born as puppies, and kittens, and foals.
Love is shadow that follows behind you.
It never leaves you alone,
But when you turn to it for the answers,
Love is the mystery. The answer's unknown.
Love is a miracle, a dream, and a gift
It steals your heart in your sleep.
Where does love hide? Where does it abide?
Nowhere else but in the depths of the sea, and your heart.

I think this was the song that Martin sang. It changes all the time, because the wind steals the words for himself as he hears it, so Martin has to make up his own song until he gets the true song back from the wind. But there is no secret to it; he knows how to catch the wind and that love is even a color hidden in the grass. Love is the secret of the heart that changes from day to night, but Martin still keeps singing about love.

SHQIPE MALUSHI

Writer, poet, performer, public speaker, empowerment coach and leadership trainer, shqipe is using storytelling to raise awareness, building leadership and peacebuilding through cross-cultural issues. Originally from Kosovo, she moved through transforming herself from an immigrant to an American.

Her stories have been published internationally, and her publications include a book of poetry "For You," in Albanian; and "The Gift of the Prophets," in English; including a manual "The Power of Change is in Your Hands!"

Her work on women's empowerment expanded beyond boundaries strengthening relationships in Afghanistan, Lebanon, Iraq, India, Kosovo, Albania and USA. She is involved in humanitarian causes, overcoming racial, cultural and religious differences. She motivates, inspires and influences a positive change through her writing and performances.

Shqipe Malushi delivers inspiring performances and moves audiences towards success. She has B.A. in Linguistics from University of Belgrade, B.A. in Writing from Sarah Lawrence College, M.A. in Performace Arts from NYU, and professional Leadership and Executive

Management Certification from Columbia University in NYC. Her stories focus on the power of love and the incredible potential of manifesting dreams.

Her honors include:

Women of Excellence, by Albanian Excellence Organization given by the President of Albania for Leadership and Peace building, New York (2016)

Iconic Women's Leadership Award for Peace building by Women's Economic Forum, New Delhi, (2016)

Recognition by the President Ashraf Ghani, of Afghanistan (2016)

Scholar in Residence Award by Institute of Government Accounts &Finance, New Delhi, India (2011)

V-Day Scholarship Award for Afghan & Indian Women's Empowerment (2011)

Paul Harris Fellow, for fostering peace and understanding among the people of the world, by Rotary International (2008)

Woman of the Year, Refugee Women's Network, Atlanta, GA (2003)

Ambassador for Peace by the Interreligious and International federation for World Peace (2003)

The Most Diverse Leader Award Certificate, by Institute for Non-Profit Management, Columbia University (2002)

North Atlantic Treaty Organization (NATO) Medal, in support of Kosovo Peacekeeping Mission (1999).

The Angel of Peace, by Women's Day Magazine (1993)